SEX TROUBLE

Essays on Radical Feminism
and the
War Against Human Nature

By Robert Stacy McCain

The Feminist Abyss

WHAT DO WE MEAN BY THE WORD "feminism"? This question has become increasingly crucial to the way that we talk about men, women and sex in the 21st century. Almost everyone claims to accept feminism if they can be permitted to define it in the most commonly accepted understanding of "equality" as basic *fairness*. Especially in terms of educational and employment opportunity, no one argues in favor of discrimination against women. Yet this widely accepted idea of feminism, as a concern for equality in the sense of fairness and opportunity, is not the goal of the feminist movement today, nor was this the goal of the movement when it began in the late 1960s. The leaders of the Women's Liberation movement were radicals – many of them were avowed Marxists – who advocated a social revolution to destroy the basic institutions of Western civilization, which they denounced as an oppressive system of male supremacy, often labeled "patriarchy." Women are oppressed and men are their oppressors, feminists declared, calling for the destruction of this systematic oppression: "Smash patriarchy!"

Feminism confuses many people who do not understand that the movement has a political philosophy – a theory – and that this theory is fundamentally incompatible with human nature. In fact, feminists do not believe there is such a thing as "human nature." Instead, they insist, all human behavior (especially including sexual behavior) is "socially constructed" and, because feminists believe that the society that constructs our behavior is a male-dominated system which oppresses women, everything that we accept as "human nature" is part of that oppressive system. A feminist blogger explained this in July 2014:

> Radical Feminism is, and has always been a political
> movement focused on liberating girls and women, those
> who are born into the sex caste female, from the unnatural,
> yet universal roles patriarchy has assigned. . . .
> Radical Feminism fights to disassemble the subliminal sex
> role behavior performances that cause female
> subordination. . . . This is socialized behavior instruction.

It's a teaching, a grooming from birth that is false, harmful
to our freedom and must stop.

What this blogger described as "the unnatural, yet universal roles
patriarchy has assigned" are the characteristics we call *masculinity*
and *femininity* – the normal traits and behaviors of men and women.
Feminists consider these roles "unnatural," both the cause and effect
of "female subordination," and their movement can therefore never
be satisfied with the simple fairness that most of us think of as
"equality." As long as these "universal roles" (masculine men and
feminine women) continue to define human existence, feminism has
not achieved its objective.

"PIV is always rape, OK?" Mocking laughter greeted this
declaration from an anonymous radical feminist blogger who, in
December 2013, explained that heterosexual intercourse — PIV
being a feminist acronym for "penis-in-vagina" — is "inherently
harmful" a manifestation of male supremacy and the patriarchy's
violent oppression of women. The same blogger elsewhere declared,
"No woman is heterosexual," a statement that seems absurd, except
to those who have studied the influential feminist scholars whose
theories support such a claim. Heterosexuality, these authors argue,
is never a woman's own free choice, nor is female heterosexuality
the result of natural instinct or biological urges. Rather, according to
radical theorists whose works are commonly taught in Women's
Studies courses at universities everywhere, women who are sexually
attracted to men have been indoctrinated — brainwashed by "hetero-
grooming" — to believe that male companionship is desirable or
necessary to their happiness.

The blogger whose anti-PIV rantings inspired so much laughter
("Was she dropped on her head?") was, in fact, able to cite as
sources for her arguments such eminent feminist authors as Mary
Daly, Dee Graham and Sheila Jeffreys. To say that these lesbian
feminists are "controversial," and that their radical views are not
shared by the majority of American women who call themselves
"feminists," is by no means a refutation of their arguments. Those
who would attempt to separate "mainstream" feminism from the
more radical aspects of its ideology cannot avoid the problem that
the faculty and curricula of university Women's Studies programs —
where feminism wields the authority of an official philosophy — are
disproportionately dominated by radical lesbians. This hegemonic
influence is not merely manifested in the fact that outspoken lesbian

activists are employed as directors and professors in Women's Studies programs everywhere, but also plainly evident in the textbooks and readings assigned in their classrooms. Even if a moderate heterosexual feminist were to become a Women's Studies professor, she would find it nearly impossible to assign a textbook that was not crammed with radical anti-male/anti-heterosexual readings from lesbian feminists like Charlotte Bunch, Adrienne Rich, Audre Lorde, Janice Raymond, Judith Butler and others.

It is this radical ideology which drives the feminist "rape culture" discourse that claims (contrary to evidence) women on college campuses are systematically victimized by male sexual violence. University administrations, state legislatures and even the federal government have reacted to these feminist claims, despite data which shows that incidents of rape have *declined* nationwide in the past two decades, and that female college students are actually *less* likely to be raped than women who don't attend college. When I covered a "SlutWalk" protest in Washington, D.C. – half-naked women marching to show that the way a woman dresses doesn't mean she is "asking for it" – I listened to their chants and realized that their message was really about silencing critics of feminism: *"Shut up, because rape."*

Feminism is a totalitarian movement that seeks to eliminate opposition by branding critics "misogynists" and "rape apologists." Attempts to discuss the actual prevalence of rape on college campuses are shouted down by feminist activists, and even after feminist claims are proven false (as when a *Rolling Stone* story about a "gang rape" at the University of Virginia was exposed as fraudulent), this doesn't end the militant rhetoric. Why? Because the "rape culture" discourse isn't about rape, *it's about culture*. It is specifically about promoting a campus culture that is hostile to men and hostile to heterosexuality. This anti-male propaganda intended to inspire in female students an attitude of hatred and suspicion toward male students: *Fear and Loathing of the Penis*.

Encountering this hateful attitude in feminist blogs, I began researching these radical theories in depth. People told me I was crazy for taking these theories seriously, but then again, I've always been crazy, and *somebody* has to pay attention to this stuff.

One reason feminism has gained so much influence in our culture is that few have been willing to confront this movement at its intellectual root, to examine the radical egalitarian theory behind feminist rhetoric. Studying dozens of books by feminist authors, I found many dangerous ideas and theories, some of them so crazy as to provoke laughter. This inspired "McCain's Law of Feminism."

There are three kinds of feminism:
1. Feminism that is wrong;
2. Feminism that is crazy;
and
3. Feminism that is both wrong *and* crazy.
When in doubt, it's usually Number Three.

Sarcasm aside, however, it's no joking matter. Feminists take their ideas very seriously, and their influence in our society – especially among the intellectual elite – means that we cannot afford to laugh them off, no matter how wrong or how crazy their ideas may be. Nor does the wrongness or insanity of their ideas mean that the problems feminists complain about are non-existent. Even if there is no "epidemic" of rape on university campuses, men *do* rape women, men *do* harass women, men *do* cheat and lie and do other bad things that hurt and harm women. The problem with feminism is that, after more than four decades, the movement has changed society in ways that actually make it more likely that women will suffer these harms. Feminists have successfully attacked basic institutions – especially marriage and the family – that should provide women protection from many of these harms. Feminists have also attacked cultural norms of morality, and undermined customs of courtesy and decency, fostering a climate where there are no commonly recognized rules to prevent or mediate conflicts between men and women. The destruction of civilized restraints has unleashed savage impulses, so that sexual relations at times approach the "war of all against all" of which Thomas Hobbes once warned.

"The personal is political," Women's Liberation leader Carol Hanisch declared in the 1960s, and this is exactly the problem with the feminist movement. These are desperately unhappy women whose grievances are so profoundly personal that attempts to solve them through politics can never succeed. Feminists are crazy, but their craziness is rooted in anger, and this anger expresses itself as the politics of revenge. For women who succumb to this ideology of insane rage, it does not matter to whether their theories are wrong or whether innocent human beings are harmed by the policies they advocate. The feminist movement demands blood sacrifice – the deaths of more than a million unborn children are destroyed annually in the name of "a woman's right to choose" – to appease their need for sadistic vengeance against the society they blame for their personal unhappiness. A movement organized with the death of innocents as one of its basic demands is not a movement that will be honest or ethical in the pursuit of its other demands. Feminism's lies are therefore never accidental or random. Rather, deliberate deception is necessary to the movement's success. Feminists lie because if they told the truth, their movement would be recognized for what it is, and would collapse in discredited failure.

When I undertook an effort to understand and explain radical feminism, my belief was that three or four months would suffice to compile my research into a book, but I was wrong. This project has already taken more than twice as long as I originally expected, and it is not finished yet. Rather than to delay publishing anything until I have completed the project, however, I have decided to publish this – a work in progress, a preview of the larger work – so that readers may begin to understand what an enormous monstrosity I've been wrestling with for these many months. We can stare together into the feminist abyss, and never forget that the abyss is staring back at us.

Robert Stacy McCain, February 22, 2015

The Long Shadow
of the 'Lavender Menace'

"The supersensitivity of the [Women's Liberation] movement to the lesbian issue, and the existence of a few militant lesbians within the movement, once prompted [NOW founder Betty] Friedan herself to grouse about 'the lavender menace' that was threatening to warp the image of women's rights."
— Susan Brownmiller, *New York Times*, March 15, 1970 (quoted in *In Our Time: Memoir of a Revolution*)

"What is a lesbian? A lesbian is the rage of all women condensed to the point of explosion. ...
"It should first be understood that lesbianism ... is a category of behavior possible only in a sexist society characterized by rigid sex roles and dominated by male supremacy. ... In a society in which men do not oppress women, and sexual expression is allowed to follow feelings, the categories of homosexuality and heterosexuality would disappear."
— Artemis March, *et al.*, Radicalesbians, "The Woman Identified Woman," May 1970

NO ONE CAN HONESTLY DISCUSS FEMINISM without addressing the enduring question, "Which feminism are you talking about?" From its inception as the Women's Liberation movement of the 1960s and '70s, modern feminism has been fractured by schisms that its would-be mainstream leaders have sought to conceal from the larger public.

Many women who today identify themselves as feminists have never examined the history of these conflicts and are unfamiliar with the militant personalities and radical ideologies that have influenced feminism for the past half-century. When confronted with the extremist rhetoric of feminists — vehement denunciation of males, condemnation of heterosexuality, claims that men (collectively) oppress and victimize women (collectively) in ways comparable to the Holocaust — the average woman is understandably startled and, if she thinks of herself as a feminist, she quickly shifts into denial mode. The anti-male passage you've just quoted to her is an aberration, an anomaly, an expression of fringe beliefs that does not represent the feminism that she endorses. *She* is not a Marxist, *she* is not a lesbian or a man-hater, *she* is not the kind of pro-abortion fanatic who views motherhood as male-imposed tyranny. The question thus arises: Is she actually a feminist?

Any honest person who undertakes an in-depth study of modern feminism, from its inception inside the 1960s New Left to its institutionalization within Women's Studies departments at universities, will understand that without the influence of radicals — militant haters of capitalism and Christianity, angry lesbians who view all males as a sort of malignant disease, deranged women who can't distinguish between political grievances and their own mental illnesses — there probably never would have been a feminist movement at all. Yet no matter how many examples of radical feminism we may cite, or how crucial the connection between ideological extremism and the rhetoric of "mainstream" feminists, many women (and men) will continue to insist that the evidence offered is irrelevant to the kind of feminism they endorse and advocate.

Unthinking acceptance of simple slogans, a superficial discourse built around glittering generalities — "equality," "choice," etc. — is not an ideology, nor could this bland kind of feminism ever have been enough to inspire an enduring political movement. Even while they ignore the chasm between radical theory and their own feminism, however, women seem surprised to find that real life contradicts even the least controversial understanding of "sexual equality." Diana Frustaci wrote in July 2014:

> I have always found it hard and confusing to be both a
> feminist and happily married. Why? Because in a good
> marriage, where both parties are equally happy, no one is
> keeping score. Feminists emphasize equality of roles, but in
> a real life marriage, this isn't always realistic.

If women make equality the measure of their happiness, they are hopelessly doomed to misery in real life, if their ambitions include men, marriage and motherhood. Somewhere, there may be a perfect

Feminist Man acceptable to the egalitarian ideal, but feminists generally mock that possibility. "Not My Nigel" is feminist shorthand for the claims of women that their man — their boyfriend, their husband, their son — does not engage in the sexist oppression that feminist rhetoric attributes to the male-dominated system of patriarchy. Feminists scorn the idea that any man can be an exception to their general condemnation of men, so that the acronym NAMALT ("Not All Men Are Like That") is deployed to ridicule any woman who takes offense at feminist claims about the ubiquitous villainy of males.

Even if a woman is certain that she herself is not being victimized by her husband, even if she refuses to accept the claim that all men are violent oppressors complicit in "rape culture," however, she will find that the routine conflicts and misfortunes of her everyday life are characterized by feminists as proof of women's universal victimhood. If she heeds the voices of feminism, she will mentally magnify her problems into evidence of a pervasive pattern, and view the men in her life — her husband, her father, her male co-workers — as participants in, and beneficiaries of, the system of "male supremacy" denounced in the 1970 manifesto, "The Woman-Identified Woman":

> Lesbian is a label invented by the Man to throw at any woman who dares to be his equal, who dares to challenge his prerogatives . . . who dares to assert the primacy of her own needs. To have the label applied to people active in women's liberation is just the most recent instance of a long history. . . For in this sexist society, for a woman to be independent means she can't be a woman — she must be a dyke. That in itself should tell us where women are at. It says as clearly as can be said: women and person are contradictory terms. For a lesbian is not considered a "real woman." . . . [W]hen you strip off all the packaging, you must finally realize that the essence of being a "woman" is to get fucked by men.

Is this brief excerpt taken out of context? Read the whole thing (it is available online in its entirety) and see for yourself if the "context" attenuates the meaning. Nor can this manifesto be dismissed as an obscure fringe document irrelevant to feminist history. It was published less than two months after Susan Brownmiller's important *New York Times* article about the nascent Women's Liberation movement had mentioned the effort of Betty Friedan to prevent "the lesbian issue" from "warp[ing] the image" of feminism. Brownmiller herself dismissed Friedan's fears, playing on the phrase "red herring" to mock the "Lavender Menace" as a "lavender herring," only to see that clever jest thrown back in her face by the collective that published its manifesto as "Radicalesbians."

"Well," replies the defender of "mainstream" feminism, *"those lesbians were just a bunch of extremist kooks nobody ever heard of."*

Except they weren't, and their kooky extremism did not hinder their influence. The "Radicalesbians" collective included Rita Mae Brown, a former staffer at Friedan's National Organization for Women. In January 1970, Brown and another lesbian NOW staffer, Michela Griffo, resigned and joined forces with Ellen Shumsky and Artemis March (*neé* March Hoffman) to form a lesbian faction within the male-dominated Gay Liberation Front. In a series of meetings in Brown's apartment, they formed a conspiracy to stage a disruptive protest as the Second Congress to Unite Women in May 1970. "The Woman-Identified Woman" was a statement largely written by March on behalf of the collective, and no one can say that either the manifesto or its authors were "fringe" obscurities. Artemis March, Ph.D., taught at Harvard University and was awarded a fellowship at the Radcliffe Institute, without ever repudiating her militant anti-male ideology. Rita Mae Brown became a best-selling author whose 1973 lesbian novel *The Rubyfruit Jungle* is often featured in high school reading lists. Ellen Shumsky became a psychotherapist; her 2009 book, *Portrait of a Decade 1968-1978*, featured an introduction by lesbian historian Flavia Rando. Michela Griffo became an artist and was recently a featured Gay Pride Month speaker in Boston.

The authors of "The Woman-Identified Woman" were not as famous as celebrity feminists like Gloria Steinem, but even if they were completely unknown, their radical manifesto would continue to be influential, because it is routinely included in the curricula of Women's Studies courses across the United States: Michigan State University, the University of Oregon, the University of Massachusetts, and the University of Minnesota, to name a few. It is not difficult to trace the influence of this early radicalism down to the present day, or to cite similarly influential treatises – *e.g.*, "Lesbians in Revolt" by Charlotte Bunch (1972) and "Compulsory Heterosexuality and Lesbian Existence" by Adrienne Rich (1980) —

commonly included in the syllabi of Women's Studies programs. Any attempt to separate this kind of explicitly anti-male/anti-heterosexual ideology from "mainstream" feminism would require us to argue that the most eminent academics in the field of Women's Studies (including the lesbian editors of the widely used textbook *Feminist Frontiers*) are not "mainstream."

Once we go beyond simplistic sloganeering about "equality" and "choice" to examine feminism as *political philosophy* — the theoretical understanding to which Ph.D.s devote their academic careers — we discover a worldview in which men and women are assumed to be implacable antagonists, where males are oppressors and women are their victims, and where heterosexuality is specifically condemned as the means by which this male-dominated system operates.

> "But the hatred of women is a source of sexual pleasure for men in its own right. Intercourse appears to be the expression of that contempt in pure form, in the form of a sexed hierarchy; it requires no passion or heart because it is power without invention articulating the arrogance of those who do the fucking. Intercourse is the pure, sterile, formal expression of men's contempt for women . . ."
> — Andrea Dworkin, *Intercourse*, 1987

> "Fucking is a large part of how females are kept subordinated to males. It is a ritual enactment of that subordination which constantly reaffirms the fact of subordination and habituates both men and women to it, both in body and in imagination."
> — Marilyn Frye, *The Politics of Reality: Essays in Feminist Theory*, 1992

> "Male supremacy is centered on the act of sexual intercourse, justified by heterosexual practice."
> — Sheila Jeffreys, interview with the *Guardian*, 2005

"Male sexual violence against women and 'normal' heterosexual intercourse are essential to patriarchy because they establish the dominance of the penis over the vagina, and thus the power relations between the sexes. . . . Men's sexual violence against women is the primary vehicle through which the dominance of the penis over the vagina is established."
— Dee Graham, *Loving to Survive: Sexual Terror, Men's Violence, and Women's Lives*, 1994

All these quotes are from authors and academics whose works are widely cited in feminist journals and included in Women's Studies curricula. To say that these feminists are outside the "mainstream" is to invite the question of who has the authority to define feminism. If lifelong activists and professors who have devoted their lives to feminism aren't "mainstream," who is? To understand this problem, consider the career of Charlotte Bunch.

In 1968, Bunch was one of the organizers of the first national Women's Liberation conference and in 1971, after being seduced by Rita Mae Brown, she divorced her husband and became a radical lesbian separatist, publishing "Lesbians in Revolt" in January 1972:

In our society which defines all people and institutions for the benefit of the rich, white male, the Lesbian is in revolt. In revolt because she defines herself in terms of women and rejects the male definitions of how she should feel, act, look, and live. To be a Lesbian is to love oneself, woman, in a culture that denigrates and despises women. The Lesbian rejects male sexual/political domination; she defies his world, his social organization, his ideology, and his definition of her as inferior. Lesbianism puts women first while the society declares the male supreme. Lesbianism . . . politically conscious and organized . . . is central to destroying our sexist, racist, capitalist, imperialist system. . . .

The only way oppressed people end their oppression is by seizing power: People whose rule depends on the

subordination of others do not voluntarily stop oppressing others. Our subordination is the basis of male power. . . . Lesbianism is a threat to the ideological, political, personal, and economic basis of male supremacy. The Lesbian threatens the ideology of male supremacy by destroying the lie about female inferiority, weakness, passivity, and by denying women's 'innate' need for men. . . .
Our rejection of heterosexual sex challenges male domination in its most individual and common form. We offer all women something better than submission to personal oppression. We offer the beginning of the end of collective and individual male supremacy. . . .
Lesbianism is the key to liberation and only women who cut their ties to male privilege can be trusted to remain serious in the struggle against male dominance.

Is that an extremist statement? Do most feminists disagree with Charlotte Bunch? Did her radical lesbianism cause her to be ostracized, marginalized and excluded from the feminist "mainstream"?

Au contraire! Charlotte Bunch became one of the most influential feminists in the world. She is a professor and founding director of the Center for Women's Global Leadership at Rutgers University. She is a top advisor to the United Nations on women's issues; she was inducted into the National Women's Hall of Fame in October 1996; and in 1999, President Clinton bestowed on her the Eleanor Roosevelt Award for Human Rights. Let us ask an obvious question:

Q. If Bunch's radical ideas are rejected by "mainstream" feminists, where are the books, articles and essays by leading feminists denouncing her as an irresponsible extremist?

A. There are no such denunciations, because the feminist movement endorses Bunch's radical anti-male ideology.

How "mainstream" is Charlotte Bunch's radicalism? In 2010, the Young Feminist Task Force promoted an International Women's Day symposium where Professor Bunch was not only a featured speaker, but the agenda included a "Tribute to Charlotte Bunch" that included a preview of the film documentary *Passionate Politics: The Life & Work of Charlotte Bunch*. Her advocacy of "rejection of heterosexual sex" as a necessary means to ending "male supremacy" is therefore not *radical* feminism or *extreme* feminism, it is simply feminism.

Nevertheless, every time feminists complain about normal women who refuse to identify themselves as feminists, it is claimed that "the negative view of feminism" as being an anti-male lesbian advocacy movement is a false stereotype rooted in ignorance. The same feminists, meanwhile, insist that one cannot oppose their radical gay agenda "unless you are part of the extremely extreme extremist right wing," as blogger Erin Matson declared in May 2013.

One almost wonders if these feminists have ever read any feminist literature, or even if they are capable of comprehending the logic of their own words. More than four decades after Artemis March and her radical comrades took up the banner of the "Lavender Menace," their rhetoric condemning "rigid sex roles and . . . male supremacy" is more influential than ever. University faculty devoted to the study of "Gender Theory" reject the categories of masculinity and femininity. What most people understand as the natural traits and normal roles of the sexes are, according to the proponents of Gender Theory, an elaborate deception into which we have been brainwashed by the anti-female, anti-gay social system called *heteronormative patriarchy*.

Such intellectual jargon strikes the normal person as ludicrous, yet it is taken so seriously on university campuses that no one who aspires to employment in academia would dare treat it as a joke.

The ferocity of campus feminists, most notoriously demonstrated by their destruction of Lawrence Summer's tenure as president of Harvard University, imposes a fearful silence within the world of higher education. Unaccustomed to criticism or opposition, academic feminists are emboldened to speak in terms of hateful extremism. Seldom does anyone even notice the poisonous quality of this rhetoric, much less object to it. One of the rare critics, Professor Daphne Patai, spent a decade teaching Women's Studies at the University of Massachusetts, and exposed the problem in her 1998 book *Heterophobia: Sexual Harassment and the Future of Feminism*:

> [M]uch of the zealotry we are seeing in the university (and
> out of it) on the issue of sexual harassment should be
> construed as an attack, quite specifically, not only on men
> but on heterosexuality itself. ... [M]en are the main target
> and ... the cessation of heterosexual expression — or even

interest — seems to be the chief agenda of many feminists.

...

[T]he standard feminist critique ... sees private
heterosexual life, and heterosexual interaction in school and
workplace, as a patriarchal imposition that must be resisted
and transformed.

What Professor Patai recognized was that feminism's rhetoric about
sexual harassment was focused entirely on condemning male
expressions of heterosexual interest in women. This was a
manifestation of the complaint in Artemis March's lesbian manifesto
that "all women are dehumanized as sex objects" by men, and of
Charlotte Bunch's celebration of lesbianism as a rejection of "the
ideology of male supremacy . . . by denying women's 'innate' need
for men."

Does heterosexuality "dehumanize" women? Has the woman who
thinks of her sexual interest in men as "innate" been brainwashed by
"the ideology of male supremacy"? Mocking laughter would be the
response of most women to such claims, and if you told them that
they had to accept such beliefs in order to escape the oppressive
impositions of patriarchy, normal women might think you were
insane.

Yet the faculty in Women's Studies departments are not normal
women, and the concept of "sexual harassment" was popularized by
a lesbian, Lin Farley, who was the first director of what became the
Women's Studies program at Cornell University.

A man who expresses romantic interest in a female has
dehumanized her as a sex object, feminism tells us, and if this male
expression of heterosexuality occurs in the workplace, the man is
guilty of sexual harassment — he has *violated her civil rights*. No
such condemnation can be made of women expressing their lesbian
interest in other women. In fact, any woman who objected to a
lesbian's sexual advances could be accused of homophobia —
possibly violating the civil rights of her lesbian pursuer!

This attitude of hostility toward heterosexuality as male
oppression of women, and the celebration of lesbianism as the
feminist ideal, has become so mainstream that we scarcely notice its
manifestations. Why was it, we may ask, that both the American
Civil Liberties Union and Florida's largest gay-rights organization
sided with lesbian sex offender Kaitlyn Hunt when it was claimed
that homophobia caused her prosecution for molesting a 14-year-old

girl ? The idea of a "lesbian loophole" in sex offender laws is startling, as is the number of recent cases in which minor girls, some as young as 12, were victimized by women teachers and coaches. The tenured radicals on university Women Studies faculties have been notably silent about such criminal cases.

Traditional morality is now routinely denounced by feminists as a "social construct" of the "heteronormative patriarchy." What has happened in the past four decades is that feminism has waged a war on human nature, and has striven (with remarkable success) to replace our normal understanding of Right and Wrong with a new system of values: Women, *good*; men, *evil*.

Thus we return to contemplate the schisms that have divided feminists since the beginning of the Women's Liberation Movement. Women who claim to endorse only "mainstream" feminism are quick to reject as a "stereotype" the image of feminists as man-hating lesbians. Yet these "mainstream" feminists refuse to criticize or condemn the influential man-hating lesbians who rule the academic world where feminist theories are promulgated. These campus radicals are not content merely to rule their collegiate domain, however. The American Association of University Women (AAUW) is now pushing to introduce "gender studies" to the high school curriculum, "creating innovative spaces for young people to engage in feminism and activism, equity, and social justice in today's classrooms." One of the leaders of this AAUW program is Ileana Jiminez, a lesbian English teacher from New York who is, among other things, an alumnus of elite Smith College, a founder of the New York Independent Schools LGBT Educators Group and a board member of the Astraea Lesbian Foundation for Justice.

Perhaps someone should tell Ms. Jiminez that her feminism is not "mainstream." Good luck with that. Feminism is no longer threatened by the Lavender Menace — now it *is* the Lavender Menace.

The Insanity of Feminism

"Women are an oppressed class. Our oppression is total, affecting every facet of our lives. We are exploited as sex objects, breeders, domestic servants, and cheap labor. . . . Our prescribed behavior is enforced by the threat of physical violence. . . .We identify the agents of our oppression as men. . . . We regard our personal experience, and our feelings about that experience, as the basis for an analysis of our common situation. We cannot rely on existing ideologies as they are all products of male supremacist culture. We question every generalization and accept none that are not confirmed by our experience."
— Redstockings, "Manifesto," July 7, 1969

"Yesterday's mental illness is today's social policy."
— Kathy Shaidle, "Feminism's Rotting Corpse," 2012

IF YOU WANT TO UNDERSTAND FEMINISM, begin by studying abnormal psychology. Perhaps no fact about the Women's Liberation movement of the 1960s and '70s is more significant than this: Shulamith Firestone, a pioneering leader of so-called "Second Wave" feminism who co-founded the radical feminist group Redstockings, was a paranoid schizophrenic who died alone at age 67, having spent decades on public assistance because of her mental illness.

Feminists can blame Firestone's pathetic fate on the oppressive patriarchy if they wish, but sane people must suspect that the cause-and-effect are quite opposite. That is to say, while feminists believe that the patriarchy makes women crazy, the rest of us suspect that *crazy women made the patriarchy* — inventing this imaginary conspiracy of "male supremacy" as the phantom menace of their paranoid minds, a fantasy bogeyman, a rationalization of their own unhappiness and misfortunes.

Here is where the meaning of the famous feminist dictum "the personal is political" exposes the real truth of their ideology. Rather than looking at feminism as a political movement to redress legitimate grievances shared generally by all women, we must understand feminism as a personal movement, concerned with the specific grievances of a distinct minority of women. To oppose feminism is not to say that the personal suffering of these women — the aggrieved minority — is not real, but rather to say that their unfortunate experiences cannot be generalized to justify a revolutionary political agenda that aims to transform society. If we change society for the benefit of the angry few, we risk destroying a society whose benefits provide happiness to the many. Feminists see no problem there; when they talk about "equality," they mean to equalize misery, too. And most feminists are profoundly miserable.

Women who are sane, normal and happy do not become feminists, because such women do not *need* feminism. Once you understand feminism as an expression of *unhappy women's psychological needs*, the general insanity of feminist doctrine makes perfect sense. This phenomenon was evident in March 2014, when a controversy arose at the University of South Carolina Upstate (USCU) because the university's Center for Women's & Gender Studies hosted Leigh Hendrix's one-woman show, "How to Be a Lesbian in 10 Days or Less."

Question: Do college girls actually need to be *told* how to be lesbians? If they are so inclined, do students at USCU (or anywhere else) lack the requisite knowledge to accomplish homosexual activity? Are they smart enough to go to college, yet too stupid to Google this stuff?

Whatever didactic purpose was served by Ms. Hendrix's performance as part of a USCU symposium called "Bodies of Knowledge," controversy flared after the event made national headlines:

> The show is a one-hour performance that follows Butchy McDyke, a motivational speaker and expert lesbian, as she "deftly guides her captive audience in an exploration of self-discovery and first love, coming out, lesbian sex, queer politics, and a really important Reba McEntire song."
> Hendrix encourages her audience to shout "I'm a big ol' dyke!" in a show that is "one part instructional seminar, one part personal story, and one part wacky performance art."

The First Amendment protects Ms. Hendrix's right to perform her show, but compelling the taxpayers of South Carolina to fund it? That is another matter altogether. South Carolina is one of the most conservative states in the country, and UCSU is in Spartanburg, in the most conservative part of the state.

Your right to shout "I'm a big ol' dyke!" does not include the right to get paid by taxpayers to shout it in a crowded theater full of college kids in Spartanburg, S.C.

Whose crazy idea was this event, anyway? The news reports about the symposium quoted Professor Lisa Johnson, the Director of the Center for Women's & Gender Studies at USCU, and so I started researching

Professor Johnson. I quickly discovered that she is — brace yourself, because I'm afraid this may shock you — a *crazy lesbian*.

Sex and the Borderline Professor

In 2010, Professor Johnson published a book about her struggles with borderline personality disorder — "a serious mental illness," according to the National Institutes for Mental Health. In her book, *Girl in Need of a Tourniquet: Memoir of a Borderline Personality,* Professor Johnson describes herself as a "psycho girlfriend" with a history of dysfunctional relationships with both men and women. Her book describes "what amounts to a nervous breakdown as the result of an affair with a married lesbian colleague." Professor Johnson in 2010 described herself as a "newlywed lesbian" whose partner was apparently her former student.

Stacey Haney was one of Professor Johnson's most honored students at USCU, receiving one of four Campus Consciousness-Raising Awards for the 2006-2007 school year and also winning an Award for Scholarly Achievement in Women's and Gender Studies for the 2007-08 school year. Professor Johnson selected the annual CWGS [Center for Women and Gender Studies] award winners in her role as the center's director. Haney served as president of the student group Upstate Feminists, and in 2008 presented a paper at the Wofford College Conference on Gender entitled, "Butch is Back: The Marginalization of Butch Feminists Across the Feminist and Queer Communities." Haney, who graduated from USCU in December 2008, subsequently served as a teaching assistant at CWGS.

Is there a law against mentally ill university professors marrying their former students? Not that I know of, not even in Spartanburg, S.C. But shouldn't the taxpayers of South Carolina have some input on who is employed to teach their daughters? And if it appears that lesbian lunatics are running the Women's Studies asylum, don't lawmakers have a fiduciary responsibility to intervene? Evidently, South Carolina legislators thought so, and eliminated the budget for USCU's Center for Women and Gender Studies in May 2014.

Gay activists may condemn South Carolina as a bastion of homophobia, but the controversy at USCU highlighted the correlation between feminism and mental illness just as much as it did the correlation between Women's Studies programs and lesbianism. Are there sane heterosexual women teaching "gender theory" at our universities? It's possible, but when you start checking the *curricula vitae* of Women's Studies professors and reading the syllabi for their classes, you gather the impression that lesbianism is both the personal and political agenda of feminism as taught and practiced on campus in the 21st century.

We may avoid speculation about the connection between homosexuality and mental illness, except to note that homosexuality was considered a mental illness *per se* until 1973, when it was eliminated from the Diagnostic and Statistical Manual in a vote of the American Psychiatric Association that was controversial at the time. There are sane lesbians, according to the APA, but just because you're gay doesn't mean you aren't also crazy, and if you spend some time examining Women's Studies textbooks, it's hard to avoid the suspicion that all the really crazy lesbians now have Ph.D.s.

Professor Sue Wilkinson and Professor Celia Kitzinger are so inseparable they share a Wikipedia entry. The British *Guardian* newspaper reported on this lesbian academic duo in March 2014:

> Eleven years after they married, two university academics celebrated becoming legally wed on Thursday, as the law in England and Wales changed to recognise same-sex marriages performed overseas.
>
> Celia Kitzinger, 57, and Sue Wilkinson, 60, who married in Canada in 2003, cracked open champagne and put on the wedding rings they had not worn in England since losing a high court battle for recognition eight years ago.
>
> As the Marriage (Same Sex Couples) Act came into force at 12.01am, other couples were for the first time able to register their intention to marry under the act, by giving statutory notice; the first ceremonies will take place on 29 March.
>
> Both Kitzinger, professor of conversation analysis, gender and sexuality at York University, and Wilkinson, professor of feminist and health studies at Loughborough University, said they had never believed legal recognition of their marriage would occur in in their lifetimes.
>
> "At midnight we were just by ourselves at a secret romantic hideaway deep in the country, and we actually opened the window of our room and we heard the bells of the local church ringing midnight," said Wilkinson. "And when the church clock went 'bong' we put on our rings and opened a bottle of champagne. It was just magical, special, lovely."

Professor Kitzinger has been "out" as a lesbian since she was a teenager, and is an editor of the journal *Feminism & Psychology*. It is scarcely an exaggeration to say that Kitzinger and Wilkinson have spent the past two decades attempting to reverse the previous psychological orthodoxy so that, among feminist scholars, it is now heterosexuality which is considered abnormal for women. This was the avowed purpose of Kitzinger and Wilkinson's 1993 book, *Heterosexuality: A Feminism & Psychology Reader*:

> The set of questions we asked [in seeking contributions to the book from feminist writers] was a deliberate reversal of those which psychology has traditionally addressed to the topic of

lesbianism: "What is heterosexuality and why is it so common? Why is it so hard for heterosexuals to change their 'sexual orientation'? What is the nature of heterosexual sex? How does heterosexual activity affect the whole of a woman's life, her sense of herself, her relationships with other women, and her political engagements?"

Citing lesbian feminist Adrienne Rich, Kitzinger and Wilkinson complain that, in much early feminist literature, "heterosexuality is simply assumed as the natural, taken-for-granted way to be for most women, obscuring the overt and covert violence with which 'compulsory heterosexuality' is forced upon us, through . . . the socialization of women to feel that male sexual 'drive' amounts to a right, the idealization of heterosexual romance, rape, pornography, seizure of children from lesbian mothers in the courts, sexual harassment, enforced economic dependence of wives and the erasure of lesbian existence from history and culture." This is quite a laundry list of grievances, and if some random woman on a street corner were to start jabbering this radical stuff in public, she'd probably be put on a 72-hour psychiatric hold. However, when these words are published in a book by a pair of tenured feminist professors, no one dare criticize their academic gibberish for fear of being condemned as a homophobe and a sexist, to boot.

Heterosexual Feminist? How Dare You!

In the introduction to their book, Kitzinger and Wilkinson describe their "entirely different experiences of heterosexuality":

[Kitzinger] has always been lesbian, came out aged 16, has never had, or wanted to have, sex with men, and developed a feminist awareness through the experience of living as a lesbian under heteropatriarchy. [Wilkinson] was happily and exuberantly heterosexual, married for 15 years, becoming lesbian only relatively recently through the impact of feminism on her emotional and sexual experience.

Does feminism cause lesbianism, or vice-versa? The answer from Kitzinger and Wilkinson seems to be, "Both." Their 1993 book may be seen in retrospect as the moment when the "Lavender Menace" — as Betty Friedan called her fear that radical lesbians would take over and discredit the feminist movement — ceased to apologize for its agenda. The lesbian takeover of feminism, especially within the academic enclaves of Women's Studies, has now progressed so far that it probably never occurred to Professor Lisa Johnson that anyone would think it weird for her to marry one of her lesbian students. Nor, perhaps, did Professor Johnson think it was unusual to stage a university symposium featuring "Butchy McDyke, a motivational speaker and expert lesbian" inciting her audience to shout "I'm a big ol' dyke!" This kind of craziness has become so commonplace within the feminist echo chamber that they don't even recognize it's crazy anymore, not even if the Republican-controlled legislature cuts off their funding.

This craziness is not recent, however, and has existed within feminism for decades. In 1993, when the lesbian academics Kitzinger and Wilkinson sent out letters seeking contributors to their book on heterosexuality, some of the responses were amusing:

> Only when we started to compile a list of heterosexual feminists as potential recipients of our letter did we realize how rare such a public identification is. It would have been much easier to compile a list of self-identified lesbian feminists. "Heterosexual" is not a popular label, and many feminists express their concern about it. . . . A couple of women we had known for years in professional contexts, who had never given us any reason to suspect that they were anything other than heterosexual . . . wrote angrily in response to our letter, "How dare you assume I'm heterosexual?" and "Don't you think you are making one hell of an assumption?"

If "heterosexual feminist" was already a rare identification in academia in the early 1990s, what does this tell us about the field of Women's Studies today? If it's practically an insult to assume a feminist is heterosexual — *"How dare you?"* — is it wrong to suspect that Women's Studies is not so much a scholarly discipline as it is a means of maximizing academic employment opportunities for lesbians?

No one is surprised to learn that Liz Sheridan, the woman who organized SlutWalk Chicago, is a Gender Studies graduate of the University of Illinois-Chicago. Parading around in your panties to protest against "rape culture" may seem crazy to normal people, but normal people don't major in Gender Studies. Normal people don't want to "Smash Patriarchy" or "F–k the System," either, but those were the mottos emblazoned on the banner leading the 2014 SlutWalk parade.

Straight, Pretty, and Abnormal

Perhaps no feminist is more famous than Gloria Steinem, the longtime editor of *Ms.* magazine. From the time she emerged as the telegenic face of the Women's Liberation movement in the early 1970s, Steinem's good looks made her the living refutation of the oft-heard claim that all feminists were fat, ugly, resentful man-haters. Steinem was not only ostentatiously attractive, she was also heterosexual, which served to refute accusations that the feminist movement was dominated by lesbians. Nevertheless, just because she was pretty and straight, it is a mistake to assume that Gloria Steinem was in any way a *typical* woman.

This point was made in a video rant by a British commentator whose online pseudonym is "Sargon of Akkad." In the video, Sargon intersperses his own comments with a television interview with Steinem. Sargon begins his YouTube rant by reading from the Wikipedia biography of Steinem:

> Steinem was born in Toledo, Ohio, on March 25, 1934. Her mother, Ruth . . . was a Presbyterian of Scottish and German descent, and her father, Leo Steinem, was the son of Jewish immigrants from Germany and Poland. The Steinems lived and traveled about in the trailer from which Leo carried out his trade as a traveling antiques dealer.
>
> When Steinem was three years old, her mother Ruth, then aged 34, had a "nervous breakdown" that left her an invalid, trapped in delusional fantasies that occasionally turned violent. She changed "from an energetic, fun-loving, book-loving" woman into "someone who was afraid to be alone, who could not hang on to reality long enough to hold a job, and who could rarely concentrate enough to read a book." Ruth spent long periods in and out of sanatoriums for the mentally disabled. Steinem was ten years old when her parents finally separated in 1944. Her father went to California to find work, while she and her mother continued to live together in Toledo.
>
> While her parents divorced as a result of her mother's illness, it was not a result of chauvinism on the father's part, and Steinem claims to have "understood and never blamed him for the breakup." Nevertheless, the impact of these events had a formative effect on her personality: while her father, a traveling salesman, had never provided much financial stability to the family, his exit aggravated their situation. Steinem interpreted her mother's inability to hold on to a job as evidence of general hostility towards working women. She also interpreted the general apathy of doctors towards her mother as emerging from a similar anti-woman animus. Years later, Steinem described her mother's experiences as having been pivotal to her understanding of social injustices. These perspectives convinced Steinem that women lacked social and political equality.

This was hardly what anyone would call a "normal" childhood, then or now, nor was Steinem typical in any other way. Steinem graduated from elite Smith College (where undergraduate tuition for the 2014-15 school year is $44,450), never had children and didn't marry until she was 66 years old. Sargon comments:

> "This is where the confusion has come in, because Gloria is not your average woman. She was raised by an insane single mother.

How could she possibly ever know what the average woman is thinking? She is clearly against the idea of the nuclear family. . . . This is exactly the problem with feminism: It goes against what women seem to actually want, and this is led by complete f–king head cases, who presume to speak for all women. She uses the term 'women this,' 'women that,' 'women the other,' as if she has spoken to all women and they had a vote — a unanimous vote for Gloria Steinem to speak for them."

Progressive Parents, Lesbian Daughters

Growing up in seriously dysfunctional families seems to be a common denominator with radical feminists. It seems that if they don't have "daddy issues," they've got "mommy issues," and the predictable attempt to blame all their "issues" on male oppression is often at odds with the available evidence. In the case of Professor Celia Kitzinger, for example, one can hardly claim that her radicalism is a reaction against her upbringing — her parents are both prominent (and predictably leftist) British intellectuals. Her father, Uwe Kitzinger, came to England as a child, a Jewish refugee from Nazi Germany, and became an economics professor, eventually head of one of the colleges at Oxford University. Her mother, Sheila Kitzinger, whose own mother was a suffragette, has been called "the high-priestess of natural childbirth," authoring a number of books on the subject, including the bestseller *The Complete Book of Pregnancy and Childbirth*. Two more progressive parents no child could ever have wished for and, in the book *Heterosexuality* she co-edited with her lesbian partner Wilkinson, Celia Kitzinger actually includes a chapter by her mother. Sheila Kitzinger writes:

I never planned to be heterosexual, of course. If I had known my three radical lesbian feminist daughters back then, I would probably never have made that decision. I just *was*. A child of patriarchy, I was shaped by it. I expected to love a man, and did. I married, made a home, had a family, established deep loyalties.

My husband Uwe and I have always shared fundamental values — values which may, just possibly, have had something to do with the fact that three of our five daughters are lesbian feminists, and that we both admire their strength and idealism. . . . [Sheila met her husband] at a meeting exploring the problems and challenges of building a better society. We were anti-racist, anti-sexist, anti-discrimination of any kind. . . . We called for world government, full employment, international understanding, world peace.

Uwe and Sheila Kitzinger sound like a perfect parody of the type of progressives who are so open-minded they believe in everything simultaneously. That three of their daughters turned out to be radical lesbian feminists doesn't seem particularly surprising. As a teenager in the 1970s, their daughter Celia was expelled from a prestigious girls' school where one of her teachers became her lesbian lover. Celia told her own story in another book, *Changing Our Minds: Lesbian Feminism and Psychology*:

> I grew up in a house full of political argument and discussion: questions of right and wrong, both in personal morality and in international politics, were fervently discussed. As children we were all encouraged to be independent and critical thinkers, to challenge taken-for-granted understandings, to question and to take stands where we believed we were in the right, "to speak truth to power." Although our sex education began at an early age and included all the details about menstruation, intercourse, conception, pregnancy, and birth, I knew nothing about lesbianism. "It just didn't occur to me that any of you would be lesbian," Sheila told me years later.
> So when, at the age of seventeen, I began my first sexual relationship with a woman, I was, despite my liberal upbringing, desperately confused and unhappy. . . .

This was circa 1974. Celia was plagued by "feelings of extreme isolation [that] led to a suicide attempt and subsequent hospitalization":

> Three months in a mental hospital, where I was diagnosed as 'immature' and 'jealous of adult sexuality,' contributed to my developing sense of psychology and psychiatry as dangerous and oppressive to lesbians.

So, naturally, she became a professor of psychology. Celia Kitzinger considers therapy harmful for women because women's problems are not personal, in her view, but rather political.

Everything must ultimately be blamed on the patriarchy, of course. It is impossible for any feminist to say otherwise. They have spent so many decades blaming every misfortune on the all-purpose scapegoat of male supremacy that one imagines the radical feminist who stubs her toe screaming in pain: "Damn the patriarchy!"

Feminism is not a political philosophy; it's an *ideé fixe*, the obsession of deranged minds. Male supremacy is to feminists what windmills were to Don Quixote or what Jews were to Hitler. This has been true since the Women's Liberation movement began, even before anyone realized that Shulamith Firestone was clinically insane. In her 1970 book *The Dialectic of Sex*, Firestone wrote this:

> So that just as to assure elimination of economic classes requires the revolt of the underclass (the proletariat) and, in a temporary

dictatorship, their seizure of the means of production, so to assure the elimination of sexual classes requires the revolt of the underclass (women) and the seizure of control of reproduction: not only the full restoration to women of ownership of their own bodies, but also their (temporary) seizure of control of human fertility — the new population biology as well as all the social institutions of child-bearing and child-rearing. And just as the end goal of socialist revolution was not only the elimination of the economic class privilege but of the economic class distinction itself, so the end goal of feminist revolution must be, unlike that of the first feminist movement, not just the elimination of male privilege but of the sex distinction itself: genital differences between human beings would no longer matter culturally. (A reversion to an unobstructed pansexuality — Freud's 'polymorphous perversity' — would probably supersede hetero/homo/bi-sexuality.) The reproduction of the species by one sex for the benefit of both would be replaced by (at least the option of) artificial reproduction: children would born to both sexes equally, or independently of. either, however one chooses to look at it; the dependence of the child on the mother (and vice versa) would give way to a greatly shortened dependence on a small group of others in general, and any remaining inferiority to adults in physical strength would be compensated for culturally. The division of labour would be ended by the elimination of labour altogether (through cybernetics). The tyranny of the biological family would be broken.

What would you call that 275-word paragraph? I call it lunatic gibberish. If you call it "political analysis," you're either a radical feminist or mentally ill — two ways of describing the same thing.

Lesbian Feminists Want to Talk to Your Daughter About Sex

CARMEN RIOS DESCRIBES HERSELF as a "raging lesbian feminist" and in 2014 she was (a) communications coordinator for the Feminist Majority Foundation, and (b) a columnist for the lesbian blog Autostraddle. On her personal Twitter account (@c_rios), she has sent out such messages as, "Do you think my mom realized that she was raising me to be the gayest person on earth?" and "If less than five percent of the population is gay, I clearly know all the gay women on earth."

On her Twitter account, Rios called herself the "Tweeter-in-Chief" for the Feminist Majority Foundation's account @Majority Speaks, which means Rios was responsible for this message:

"A new study says #realsexed should begin for kids as early as age ten -- when our sexual identities begin to emerge."

That message linked a blog post at the Feminist Majority Foundation's site, which cited a study that claims: "Children should begin receiving formal education about sexual health as early as age 10" because "sexuality and gender identity begin emerging between the ages of 10 and 14." It's important to reach kids while they are "still malleable," the researchers said:

"If programs, based on the healthy adolescent framework, rooted in human rights and gender equity, are implemented at a time when adolescents are still malleable and relatively free of sexual and reproductive health problems and gender role bias, very young adolescents can be guided safely through this life stage, supported by their parents, families and communities."

Hmmm. They want to target these programs, based on "gender equity," at kids who "are still malleable and relatively free of . . . gender role bias." What do you think those terms "gender equity" and "gender role bias" mean? And why are Carmen Rios and the Feminist Majority Foundation so excited about this? If you were a suspicious type of person, you might wonder about such things.

People sometimes ask me, "Stacy, where do you find this crazy stuff?" In this case, I was looking for some information about university Women's Studies programs and — thank you, Carmen

Rios! — encountered a very interesting Autostraddle article entitled "Rebel Girls: The Illustrated (And Quite Condensed) History of Women's Studies." Among other things, Ms. Rios reported in that article:

> *Ms.* magazine found that over 900 programs in the women's studies field were functioning in the US in 2009. That meant 10,000 courses teaching over 90,000 students at 700 colleges and universities across the nation were fueling critical thought on gender, class, race and sexuality. That included 31 Master's programs and 13 Ph.D. programs across the country and the world.

This was the information I was looking for — data on the number of Women's Studies programs and their enrollment — and it is further helpful to know that (a) Ms. magazine is published by the Feminist Majority Foundation, and (b) this research about Women's Studies was done "with generous support from the Ford Foundation." However, Carmen Rios' article at Autostraddle did not merely chronicle the history and provide statistical data about Women's Studies. She included this bit of colorful commentary:

> In the early 2000s, academics across the discipline grappled with a title for their field. . . . Is it Gender Studies? Women's Studies? Women's And Gender Studies? Sexuality Studies? Gender and Sexuality Studies? LGBT Studies? Queer Studies? Feminist Studies? . . .
> Coursework in a women's studies class today might cover issues of race, sexuality, gender expression and identity, sexualization and socialization of women, global women's rights and various international diaspora, history, art or peace. Women's Studies remains an interdisciplinary field, making its name all the more difficult to decide on. Is it Women's History and Theory, or is the program really Lesbo Recruitment 101?

She said that, not me, although it is helpful to have — from the communications coordinator of the Feminist Majority Foundation, no less — such a frank admission of the not-so-hidden agenda in Women's Studies as it is generally taught on American college campuses. And obviously, "the personal is the political" for Carmen Rios:

Women's Studies Saved My Life,
And I Want It To Change Yours, Too

I think women's studies saved my life, but I don't know what that means. Maybe that I'm not good at anything else – that I failed at being normal, that I failed at falling into line, that I failed at being everyone else, that I'll never talk to God. . . .

(This is another possible definition of "feminist" — a woman who has "failed at being normal.")

When I was 17, I took my first women's studies class. I was still in high school, but I had elected to take courses at the local community college. . . .

(Got to reach 'em early, you see.)

The woman at the helm of this experience was named Bonnie. "I try to remain impartial about most things," she told us, "except for two: Ronald Reagan and Phyllis Schafly."

That was when everything changed. . . .

(Not that there's any political agenda *involved, you see.)*

I was raised a feminist — albeit one who, before this class, knew almost nothing of my foremothers or the movement I would come to call home. . . .

Then one day, I was 17, and Hillary Clinton was running for President, and every day I would eat yogurt with granola at the café in the student center and swing my legs while I read from our textbooks for my course. I started to realize how connected I was to something so much larger than myself, and how important it was for me to recognize that, to own it, to live it. . . . This one course had shifted my core. It had shattered my entire understanding of the world.

. . .

For me, the rest is herstory: I graduated high school, became a women's studies major and a raging lesbian feminist in college, and moved into the non-profit sector. I went into that movement and never came back out — and now, I do my best in my professional life to bring it to everyone else.

How many times do I have to repeat it? *Feminism is a journey to lesbianism.* Women's Studies is a vehicle for that journey, as Carmen Rios is honest enough to admit. It's interesting to see how prominent she was as a student at American University in 2011, when an article in the campus newspaper reported:

You've definitely heard her name around campus or at least
seen her and her hard-to-miss hairdo crossing the quad on a
mission. Frankly, if you haven't, you don't even go here.
Carmen Rios, current director of Women's Initiative (WI)
is a staple on American University's campus. She's got
wild hair and a feisty attitude to match. . . .

Carmen was a big part of Slut Walk DC back in the summer
[of 2011] and even spoke at the event! Because she came to
DC, she was able to nail awesome internships like Holla
Back DC!, a grassroots organization aimed at ending sexual
harassment and assault in DC. As well as the Institute for
Women's Policy Research, which conducts research geared
toward the needs of women to promote public dialog, and
the Feminist Majority Foundation (FMF), which promotes
women's equality and empowerment. . . .

Keep an eye out for some study breaks and big events this
spring from Women's Initiative! They'll be hosting The
Vagina Monologues, celebrating Women's History Month
in March, and, of course, Take Back the Night will take
place in April again.

There are two words you won't find in that feature profile: "gay" or
"lesbian." Why would this campus publication omit these terms from
an article about the student director of American University's
Women's Initiative, when she herself identified as a "raging
lesbian"? Never mind. The more relevant point is her involvement
with events like Slut Walk DC and "Take Back the Night," both of
which are about rape. Campus activism about rape provides a means
of disseminating the core message of feminist ideology, *i.e.*, that
men are evil and dangerous and that male sexuality is inherently
violent and oppressive to women. She won an award for this:

Carmen Rios, current Director of Women's Initiative, was
the co-recipient of the Feminist Research Award for her
efforts to end sexual violence on college campuses. Rios
says, "the topic of sexual violence is consistently relevant to
college-aged women, since one out of every four
undergraduate women will experience sexual assault."

This "one out of every four" claim is a phony statistic lacking
empirical support. But who needs facts when you've got an
ideology?

As anti-rape strategies go, becoming a "raging lesbian feminist in college" could arguably be effective, which may be why lesbian feminists so frequently lament that their numbers are so few. According to a Huffington Post survey in 2013, only 18 percent of women identify themselves as feminists, and only 5 percent call themselves "strong" feminists. By a 32-29 margin, a larger percentage of women consider "feminist" a negative term than a positive term. And despite decades of gay activism, about 98 percent of women are heterosexual, according to government research.

Fanatical ideologues are not easily deterred, however. If decades of campus activism aimed at turning college girls into man-haters — Women's Studies as "Lesbo Recruitment 101," as Ms. Rios calls it — have so far failed to have the intended effect, then obviously they need to reach girls at an earlier age. There might be some parental resistance, of course, if these radicals were honest, showing up at your local elementary school and declaring: *"Hi, we're lesbian feminists and we're here to talk to your daughter about sex."*

Instead, the American Association of University Women has started advocating to implement "gender studies" programs in public high schools, and the Feminist Majority Foundation is enthusiastic about the prospect of teaching 10-year-olds about "sexuality and gender identity" with a focus on "gender equity" while girls "are still malleable and relatively free of . . . gender role bias."

When I published an article about Carmen Rios in August 2014, her colleagues at Autostraddle freaked out, accusing me of having written a "hit piece." Feminists evidently consider it a hate crime to quote them, but what Ms. Rios wrote – how she personally became a "raging lesbian feminist" after taking a Women's Studies class – was entirely consistent with what I'd learned in my research about radical feminist theory. The Women's Studies curriculum at most universities is anti-male and anti-heterosexual, and the correlation between these three variables — radical feminism, lesbianism, and Women's Studies programs — is a phenomenon worthy of critical scrutiny.

This connection gets so little scrutiny simply because anyone who calls attention to the truth about feminist theory can expect to be attacked as a misogynist, and critics of feminism are effectively banned from university campuses. This is why most people don't understand that academic feminism has become vehemently hostile to heterosexuality in recent decades. *Feminists deny that heterosexuality is natural*, insisting that it is "imposed" on women by "male power," as Adrienne Rich notoriously argued in 1980:

> Some of the forms by which male power manifests itself are more easily recognizable as enforcing heterosexuality on women than are others. Yet each one . . . adds to the cluster of forces within which women have been convinced that marriage and sexual orientation toward men are inevitable, even if unsatisfying or oppressive components of their lives. . . .
>
> The assumption that "most women are innately heterosexual" stands as a theoretical and political stumbling block for many women. . . . [T]o acknowledge that for women heterosexuality may not be a 'preference' at all but something that has had to be imposed, managed, organized, propagandized and maintained by force is an immense step to take if you consider yourself freely and "innately" heterosexual. Yet the failure to examine heterosexuality as an institution is like failing to admit that the economic system called capitalism or the caste system of racism is maintained by a variety of forces, including both physical violence and false consciousness.

If heterosexuality is "maintained by force," as Rich argued, then how can it be said that *any* woman genuinely consents to sex with men? This is a deliberate insult to normal men and women, and Rich's essay has become part of the core curriculum in Women's Studies programs across the country. This radical ideology, rather than bland slogans about "equality," is what comprises feminism as it is taught to the tens of thousands of college students enrolled in these college and university classes.

From the feminist point of view, the woman who has a husband and children is being cruelly oppressed by the patriarchy, a conspiratorial apparatus of male supremacy. According to the best available data, about 98% of Americans are heterosexual, yet the expectations of normal parents that their children will also be normal are condemned by feminists as a type of harmful prejudice called *heteronormativity*. These core doctrines of radical feminism are not new, nor are these "fringe" beliefs within the feminist movement. The most widely assigned anthology of feminist literature, used as an introductory text in many Women's Studies programs, is edited by three lesbian professors, and syllabi for Women's Studies classes routinely include assignments of anti-male/anti-heterosexual writings by such radical authors Charlotte Bunch, Sheila Jeffreys, Andrea Dworkin, Janice Raymond and Mary Daly. One cannot effectively oppose an ideology one does not understand. We are in a Culture War that began long ago and far away, as Linda Kimball explained in a 2007 article for American Thinker:

> In 1919, Georg Lukacs became Deputy Commissar for Culture in the short-lived Bolshevik Bela Kun regime in Hungary. He immediately set plans in motion to de-Christianize Hungary. Reasoning that if Christian sexual ethics could be undermined among children, then both the hated patriarchal family and the Church would be dealt a crippling blow. Lukacs launched a radical sex education program in the schools. Sex lectures were organized and literature handed out which graphically instructed youth in free love (promiscuity) and sexual intercourse while simultaneously encouraging them to deride and reject Christian moral ethics, monogamy, and parental and church authority. All of this was accompanied by a reign of cultural terror perpetrated against parents, priests, and dissenters.

The phenomenon originated by Lukacs, Cultural Marxism, is generally today known as political correctness, and its objective has never changed. The goal is to destroy Christianity, and with it the "bourgeois morality" that Marxists understood as the cultural underpinning of Western democratic capitalist society. Once we understand feminism in the larger context of Cultural Marxism, we recognize that (a) bland slogans like "equality," "choice" and "progress" are not the actual agenda; (b) the actual agenda involves the wholesale destruction of Western civilization; and (c) the people involved in advancing this agenda are the enemies of all humanity.

It is easy enough to laugh at these people as kooks, but the startling fact is that radical feminists exercise such influence on American university campuses that no one within academia dares oppose them, as was illustrated when Lawrence Summers was hounded out of office as president of Harvard University for merely suggesting that there may be "innate" differences between men and women. The fact that Carmen Rios became an award-winning student leader as a "raging lesbian feminist" in American University's Women's Studies program is a rather large clue as to what is being taught in that program. And the fact that Ms. Rios went onto a post-graduate career as communications coordinator for the Feminist Majority Foundation (annual budget $6.5 million) indicates that such radicalism is welcomed within "mainstream" feminism.

Who sponsors the annual Young Feminist Conference in D.C.? The Feminist Majority Foundation. And who was moderator of the 2014 conference's digital communications panel discussion? Carmen Rios. So when college girls want to learn how to promote feminism online, it's the "raging lesbian feminist" who teaches them.

Why is it a "hit piece" simply to point out that Carmen Rios lives a life consistent with her beliefs? Feminism teaches young women that men are their enemies and that heterosexuality is a weapon of male supremacy. It is therefore impossible to imagine why any woman who subscribes to feminist ideology would be interested in a normal life of men, marriage and motherhood. Even if she were able to reconcile her anti-male belief system with a sexual interest in men, no feminist could ever be *happy* in such a relationship, even stipulating that any man would be interested in a relationship with her.

That feminism is incompatible with heterosexuality is obvious to lesbian bloggers who do not hesitate to denounce the normal woman as being a man's "fuckhole," a "dick socket," a "breeder." And from the feminist point of view, this contempt for heterosexuality is entirely rational, justified by their theory of patriarchy. If indeed women's condition is one of cruel oppression and unfair subordination, a condition imposed upon them by the selfishness of men, no man can ever possibly be worthy of the admiration and respect of any woman. Male erotic interest in women is, according to feminist ideology, the basic cause of women's "humiliation" as inferiors. The man who desires a woman as his sexual partner only wishes to subject her to an "inherently violent" act.

Such is the feminist view of men, of heterosexual relationships, of normal marriage and motherhood. If you are a woman who actually desires those things (romance, a wedding, a husband and children, a family home) then *you are not a feminist.* You may call yourself a "feminist," but it's impossible to reconcile a normal female life with the radical project of overthrowing the patriarchy. And if you're a woman committed to overthrowing patriarchy (*i.e.*, reducing men to the status of passive drones in a sexless androgynous regime of "equality" where men are only acceptable if they display a masochistic appetite for the companionship of women who despise them), it's impossible to imagine how you could ever experience sexual desire toward whatever pathetic males might choose this fate to which feminism would condemn them.

Thus we return to Carmen Rios, the "raging lesbian feminist" who is not afraid to joke that Women's Studies classes function as "Lesbo Recruitment 101" seminars for many young women. Her comrades at Autostraddle condemned me for writing a "hit piece" about Ms. Rios, when all I had done was to discuss her career and opinions as a typical example of feminist ideology in operation.

This is all consistent with the doctrines of pioneering lesbian feminist theorists who condemned the idea of heterosexuality as an "innate" or "natural" expression of female sexuality. Equality for women was only possible if they could be liberated from the constraints of what Rich called "compulsory heterosexuality." What scientists had claimed were "natural" sexual instincts, these eminent feminist writers explained, were actually the product of social pressures and cultural beliefs imposed on women by the system of male supremacy. Daphne Patai has described how feminism theorizes this process:

> Dee Graham . . . claims to be able to explain the very existence of heterosexuality in women by invoking what she calls the "Societal Stockholm Syndrome." In a 1994 book entitled *Loving to Survive*, Graham expounds her theory in minute detail. As in the famous Stockholm bank-hostage episode in 1973, in which four hostages bonded with their captors and came to see the police as their common enemy, women — so the argument goes — are eternally held hostage to men. . . . The point of all male behavior is domination . . . Heterosexual behavior thus becomes a "survival strategy" for women, as do "feminine" characteristics, which result from women's need to ingratiate themselves with their "captors." . . .
> Graham's thesis makes it impossible to distinguish in a meaningful way between situations of genuine abuse and the ordinary life of heterosexual women. And that is precisely the point. Men are women's captors. Women are men's hostages. Heterosexuality is the form of their subjugation.

As extreme as Graham's claims may seem, this kind of "subjugation" is what feminists mean when they condemn our society and culture by labeling it "male supremacy" and "patriarchy." The feminist goal of overthrowing patriarchy requires the abolition of heterosexuality and, as Carmen Rios clearly understands, this project will require an active campaign of "education" in schools to eradicate the *heteronormative oppression* of girls while their emerging sexual identity is "still malleable."

That the logic of feminist theory is obvious in this regard, however, does not mean either (a) that all women who call themselves "feminists" have followed the premises of their syllogism to a logical conclusion, or (b) that all women who understand the esoteric doctrine of feminism are willing to discuss it with the larger public outside the inner circle of their cult. It follows from this — *i.e.*, the necessary disconnect between feminism's *esoteric* doctrine and feminism's *exoteric* discourse — that there are many women who earnestly support what they believe to be "feminism" without having any knowledge of the etiology and teleology of the movement's fundamental ideology.

Disney Movies:
Heteronormative Oppression?

IS YOUR DAUGHTER A VICTIM of male oppression? Blame *Aladdin* — as well as *The Little Mermaid, Pocahontas, The Lion King* and *Toy Story 2*. Disney cartoons and other G-rated children's movies are full of "gendered sexuality," subjecting women to the male "objectifying gaze," as "heterosexuality is constructed through hetero-romantic love relationships as exceptional, powerful, magical, and transformative."

These were the conclusions of Women's Studies professors Karin Martin and Emily Kazyak in their 2009 research paper, "Hetero-Romantic Love and Heterosexiness in Children's G-Rated Films." The sociologists examined "all the G-rated films grossing $100 million dollars or more between 1990 and 2005" and found that these movies convey what feminists call "heteronormativity":

> Heteronormativity includes the multiple, often mundane
> ways through which heterosexuality overwhelmingly
> structures and "pervasively and insidiously" orders
> "everyday existence" . . . Heteronormativity structures
> social life so that heterosexuality is always assumed,
> expected, ordinary, and privileged. Its pervasiveness makes
> it difficult for people to imagine other ways of life. . . .
> Anything else is relegated to the nonnormative, unusual,
> and unexpected and is, thus, in need of explanation.
> Specifically, within heteronormativity, homosexuality
> becomes the "other" against which heterosexuality defines
> itself. . . .
> Heteronormativity regulates those within its boundaries as
> it marginalizes those outside of it. . . .
> Heteronormativity also rests on gender asymmetry, as
> heterosexuality depends on a particular type of normatively
> gendered women and men.

The feminist critique of heteronormativity and gender roles dates back to the earliest years of the Women's Liberation Movement (so-called "second-wave" feminism) of the 1960s and '70s. Radical lesbian manifestos denounced heterosexuality as part of a "sexist society characterized by rigid sex roles and dominated by male supremacy," which "denigrates and despises women," where women's "subordination" as inferiors is central to a "sexist, racist, capitalist, imperialist system."

Feminism's anti-male theories were further advanced by Adrienne Rich's influential 1980 essay, "Compulsory Heterosexuality and Lesbian Existence," which has been so widely cited that lesbian scholars like Professor Judith Butler invoke Rich's phrase "compulsory heterosexuality" without bothering to credit its originator.

Martin and Kazyak's critique of heteronormativity and gender roles in children's movies relies on the work of radical feminists, including Gayle Rubin, a controversial lesbian activist whose treatise "Thinking Sex: Notes for a Radical Theory of the Politics of Sexuality" is cited as authority for how heterosexuality is part of a system of "inequalities, like race and class, [that] intersect and help construct what Rubin calls 'the inner charmed circle' in a multitude of complicated ways." Readers of Rubin's 1984 essay may be shocked to learn that she favorably cited the pedophile group NAMBLA (North American Man/Boy Love Association) in opposition to laws against child pornography:

> For over a century, no tactic for stirring up erotic hysteria has been as reliable as the appeal to protect children. The current wave of erotic terror has reached deepest into those areas bordered in some way, if only symbolically, by the sexuality of the young. . . . In February 1977 . . . a sudden concern with 'child pornography' swept the national media. In May, the Chicago Tribune ran a lurid four-day series with three-inch headlines, which claimed to expose a national vice ring organized to lure young boys into prostitution and pornography. Newspapers across the country ran similar stories, most of them worthy of the National Enquirer. By the end of May, a congressional investigation was underway. Within weeks, the federal government had enacted a sweeping bill against 'child pornography' and many of the states followed with bills of their own. . . .
>
> The laws produced by the child porn panic are ill-conceived and misdirected. They represent far-reaching alterations in the regulation of sexual behaviour and abrogate important sexual civil liberties. But hardly anyone noticed as they

swept through Congress and state legislatures. With the exception of the North American Man/Boy Love Association and American Civil Liberties Union, no one raised a peep of protest.

It is perhaps unnecessary to point out the ironic contradiction: In 1984, Gayle Rubin was citing NAMBLA to denounce a "child porn panic" as a menace to "important sexual civil liberties"; twenty-five years later, Rubin's radical treatise was cited by two university Women's Studies professors who see G-rated children's films as a menace.

"Don't worry about perverts and kiddie porn, Mom. It's those heteronormative Disney movies that are the real danger!"

The "erotic terror" Karin Martin and Emily Kazyak want to protect girls from is heterosexuality and normal gender roles portrayed in movies like *Aladdin, Pocahontas* and *Beauty and the Beast*:

These films repeatedly mark relationships between cross-gender lead characters as special and magical by utilizing imagery of love and romance. Characters in love are surrounded by music, flowers, candles, magic, fire, ballrooms, fancy dresses, dim lights, dancing, and elaborate dinners. Fireflies, butterflies, sunsets, wind, and the beauty and power of nature often provide the setting for — and a link to the naturalness of — hetero-romantic love. For example, in Beauty and the Beast, the main characters fall in love frolicking in the snow; Aladdin and Jasmine fall in love as they fly through a starlit sky in Aladdin; Ariel falls in love as she discovers the beauty of earth in The Little Mermaid; . . . Pocahontas is full of allusion to water, wind, and trees as a backdrop to the characters falling in love. The characters often say little in these scenes. Instead, the scenes are overlaid with music and song that tells the viewer more abstractly what the characters are feeling. These scenes depicting hetero-romantic love are also paced more slowly with longer shots and with slower and soaring music.

These films also construct the specialness of hetero-romantic love by holding in tension the assertion that hetero-romantic relationships are simultaneously magical and natural. In fact, their naturalness and their connection to "chemistry" and the body further produce their exceptionalness. . . . These formulations include ideas about reproductive instincts and biology, and they work to naturalize heterosexuality. We see similar constructions at work in these G-rated movies where the natural becomes the magical. These films show that, in the words of Mrs. Pots from Beauty and the Beast, if "there's a spark there," then all that needs to be done is to "let nature take its course."

Translation: *"Damn those patriarchal oppressors and their hateful heteronormative 'ideas about reproductive instincts and biology'!"*

This kind of gender-theory deconstruction of popular culture is now ubiquitous in Women's Studies programs, and it is certainly no accident that the most widely used anthology of feminist literature is edited by three lesbian professors. Academic feminists are hostile to any claim that heterosexual attraction is natural. If you consider sexual desire and romantic love between men and women to be natural and healthy, you are not a feminist. There is nothing natural about sex, according to feminist ideology, no biological urge that causes women to be attracted to men.

Because feminists view heterosexuality as intrinsic to "male supremacy," they argue that women's romantic interest in men is "socially constructed" — a delusion imposed on women by patriarchal brainwashing — and Karin Martin blames mothers for encouraging girls to be heterosexual. In the anti-Disney screed she co-authored with Kazyak, Martin cited her own research from another 2009 paper titled "Normalizing Heterosexuality: Mothers' Assumptions, Talk, and Strategies with Young Children."

Obviously, mothers are letting their daughters watch Disney movies as part of these "strategies" to teach their girls how to be victims of male heterosexual oppression. Being beautiful, so as to attract "the male gaze" as sex objects, is what Martin and Kazyak condemn as the "heterosexiness" of female cartoon characters:

Heteronormativity requires particular kinds of bodies and interactions between those bodies. Thus, as heterosexuality is constructed in these films, gendered bodies are portrayed quite differently, and we see much more of some bodies than others. Women throughout the animated features in our sample are drawn with cleavage, bare stomachs, and bare legs. . . .

[In the 1996 Disney feature *The Hunchback of Notre Dame*] Quasimodo accidentally stumbles into Esmeralda's dressing area, and she quickly covers up with a robe and hunches over so as not to expose herself. She ties up her robe as Quasimodo apologizes again and again and hides his eyes. However, as he exits, he glances back toward her with a smile signifying for the viewer his love for her. A glimpse of her body has made her even more lovable and desirable. . . .

[W]omen's bodies become important in the construction of heteronormative sexuality through their "sexiness" at which men gaze. Much of the sexuality that these gendered bodies engage in has little to do with heterosexual sex narrowly defined as intercourse or even behaviors that might lead to it, but rather with cultural signs of a gendered sexuality for women.

So, for all these years American parents thought their daughters were just watching kiddie cartoons, when instead these Disney movies are actually part of how "heterosexuality is constructed" by the patriarchy to impose "gendered sexuality" on little girls. Please, professors, tell us more about this animated misogynistic oppression:

The best example of the representation of sexiness appears in *The Hunchback of Notre Dame*. Esmeralda, the Gypsy female lead, is drawn with dark hair, big green eyes, a curvy body, cleavage, and a small waist. She is also drawn with darker skin than other lead Disney characters like Belle (*Beauty and the Beast*) and Ariel (*Little Mermaid*). Darker skin and hair and "exotic" features are part of the representation of heterosexual sexiness for women. Moreover, Esmeralda spends much time in this film swaying her hips and dancing "sexily" while men admire her.

Not all scenes with the signification of sexiness are so elaborated. When the candlestick and duster are turned back into people in *Beauty and the Beast*, the now-voluptuous maid prances bare-shouldered in front of the chef who stares. Throughout *Aladdin*, especially in fast-paced musical scenes, sexy women prance, preen, bat their eyelashes, shake their hips, and reveal their cleavage. When Genie sings to Aladdin, he produces three women with bare stomachs and bikini-like outfits who dance around him, touch him, bat their eyes at him, and kiss him. He stares at them sometimes unsure, but wide-eyed and smiling. When Prince Ali comes to ask Princess Jasmine for her hand in marriage, his parade to the castle is adorned with writhing, dancing women with bare stomachs and cleavage. Later, Jasmine sees Prince Ali as a fraud and tricks him with similarly sexy moves. Heterosexiness in *Aladdin* is delivered through the bodies of women of color who are exoticized.

Translation: *"Those heteronormative Disney oppressors aren't just sexist, they're racist, too! How dare they 'exoticize' women of color!"*

This is perhaps a good place to mention that Christian conservatives — despite our hateful enthusiasm for patriarchy — have frequently criticized the messages embedded in Disney products. Often, the same "hetero-erotic" themes that offend feminists offend conservatives, but for different reasons. Youthful rebellion against parental authority by the pursuit of forbidden love is fairly common in these movies. Ariel's romance in *The Little Mermaid* is a rebellion against her father Poseidon, and forbidden romances are also central to the stories in *Pocahontas* and *Aladdin*. The use of magic — which Bible-believers must condemn as sorcery and witchcraft — is another common Disney plot device. (Did you say "Magic Kingdom"? And do we know who rules this kingdom, boys and girls? Satan!) *Pocahontas* is particularly egregious to conservative sensibilities, depicting English colonists as violent, greedy predators, while portraying the natives as peaceful proto-environmentalists who live in harmony with nature. Any conservative Christian theologian would see the "mystical" elements in Pocahontas as a celebration of pagan nature-worship.

Likewise, the "heterosexiness" that Martin and Kazyak view through the prism of gender theory is offensive to many conservative parents, although for different reasons. Conservatives don't think their daughters should have to bare their cleavage or make "sexy moves" to attract male interest. Nor, for that matter, do conservatives think that our daughters are apt to find healthy relationships by becoming slaves to "chemistry" and acting on every magical "spark" that might persuade them to "let nature take its course." Mature adults understand that "chemistry" — especially wild hormonal impulses of adolescence — can often lead young people to irresponsible and reckless behavior. Whether we are Christians who oppose fornication on moral grounds, or rationalists who wish our children to learn responsible restraint on their potentially harmful erotic impulses, conservative parents reject permissive attitudes about letting children pursue their "feelings" and "instincts" in romance.

Paradoxes abound when comparing feminist and conservative critiques of popular culture. Martin and Kazyak condemn the heteronormative "gendered sexuality" expressed by the costumes and gestures of female Disney characters. Most traditionalist parents would be appalled if their daughters dressed and behaved like the *Hunchback*'s Esmerelda, *Aladdin*'s Jasmine or *The Little Mermaid*. ("If you think you're leaving the house dressed like that, Ariel, you've got another think coming! Wearing those seashells like a little beach tramp! Now march yourself back upstairs and put on a sweater, young lady!") While it is acceptable for two Women's Studies professors to condemn the "heterosexiness" of Disney princesses, however, any conservative who criticized these characters' cleavage-bearing outfits would be denounced by feminists for engaging in "slut-shaming."

The question of whether Disney cartoon features are entirely "family friendly" in one that thoughtful conservatives have often discussed. Yet the parts of these G-rated movies that are most wholesome, from a conservative perspective, are predictably singled out for criticism by the feminist professors Martin and Kazyak:

> [T]here is much explicit heterosexual gazing at or ogling of women's bodies in these films. . . .
>
> When the main characters refrain from overt ogling and sexual commentary, the "sidekicks" provide humor through this practice. For example, in *Toy Story 2*, Rex, Potato Head, Slinky Dog, and Piggy Bank drive through aisles of a toy store and stop at a "beach party" where there are many Barbies in bathing suits, laughing and dancing. As the male characters approach, a jackpot sound ("ching") is heard, and all four male characters' jaws drop open. Then "Tour Guide Barbie" acrobatically lands in their car and says she will help them. They all stare at her with open eyes and mouths. Mr. Potato Head recites again and again, "I'm a married spud, I'm a married spud, I'm a married spud," and Piggy

Bank says, "Make room for single fellas" as he jumps over Potato Head to sit next to Barbie. They remain mesmerized by Barbie as she gives them a tour of the store.

Anyone who has seen *Toy Story 2* — at least, anyone except lesbian Women's Studies professors — knows that this is one of the funniest scenes in the whole movie. The reactions of the four male characters are so funny because they are so true-to-life. And the reaction of Mr. Potato Head, reminding himself that he is married when unexpectedly finding himself seated next to vivacious young "Tour Guide Barbie," is exactly what any Christian pastor — or any wife, for that matter — would expect a married man to do in such a situation. If only Bill Clinton had remembered he was a "married spud," the Monica Lewinsky scandal and Clinton's impeachment could have been avoided.

Marital loyalty requires that both husbands and wives strive to resist the temptations of "heterosexiness," but this obligation — a sacred duty, as Christians would say — is most often breached by men. Bill Clinton certainly wasn't the first middle-aged married man to discover that career success could be leveraged as sexual access to misguided young women for whom male power had the effect of an aphrodisiac. This is not to deny that the reverse scenario occurs, as when female teachers like Mary Kay LeTourneau and Debra Lafave engage in illegal sex with underage males. However, for every sex-crazed female "cougar" stalking young male prey, there have always been many more married men willing to take advantage of foolish young women. In fact, this was the subject of one of the most famous musical quarrels in history. Hank Thompson had a Number One country hit in 1952 with this lament:

I never knew God made honky-tonk angels.
Should have known you would never make a wife.
You have lost the only one who ever loved you,
And went back to the wild side of life.

To that, Kitty Wells famously replied with her own Number One hit:

It wasn't God who made honky-tonk angels,
As you wrote in the words of your song.
Too many times married men think they're still single.
That has caused many a good girl to go wrong.

Amen, sister! Complaints about double-standards and an endless finger-pointing blame game in the War of the Sexes long pre-dated the rise of the feminist movement, and there is more wisdom in those Grand Ole Opry classics than in all the "gender theory" treatises ever published by Women's Studies professors. The true classics in our popular culture endure over time precisely because they reflect important truths about human nature. Take it away, Elvis:

Well, a hard-headed woman,
A soft-hearted man,
Been the cause of trouble
Ever since the world began. . . .
Samson told Delilah
Loud and clear,
"Keep your cotton pickin' fingers
Out of my curly hair!"
Oh yeah, ever since the world began,
A hard-headed woman been
A thorn in the side of man.

Is that song an example of patriarchal heteronormative misogyny? Certainly. Why do you think they called him the "King," huh? We laugh as we imagine the feminist critique of old rock-and-roll songs, but Ph.D.s in Women's Studies expect to be taken seriously when they tell us Disney cartoons are part of a male-supremacy plot to brainwash girls into becoming heterosexual. But nothing would horrify parents more than if their daughter were to become "heterosexual" in the generic sense — that is to say, becoming sexually available to *all* men.

Strippers, porn performers, and prostitutes are "heterosexual" in that sense, and yet it is conservatives, not feminists, who most frequently criticize women's degradation in what is euphemistically called "sex work." Conservatives are condemned for "slut-shaming" — and Republicans are accused of waging a "War on Women" — when they criticize the reckless promiscuity defended by many feminists.

Duke University Women's Studies major Miriam Weeks ("Belle Knox") became famous in 2014 by insisting it is an "empowering" expression of her "sexual autonomy" for her to perform oral sex, let men ejaculate on her face, and be penetrated every possible way in the teen porn videos where she is paid to endure sexual humiliation. Miriam Weeks is not strictly heterosexual, and has enacted numerous lesbian scenes in her brief porn career. She describes herself as bisexual and has said she started watching porn videos when she was 11 or 12. By the time she was a college freshman, the Duke feminist told one interviewer, she was already so jaded she could only "get off" watching videos in which females perform oral sex on men.

Like the old song says, it wasn't God who made honky-tonk angels. And whatever academic feminists may theorize, it isn't Disney movies that turn girls into pathetic creatures like Miriam Weeks.

Essential Feminist Quotes

ONE OF THE PERSISTENT PROBLEMS faced by critics of feminism is that the core concepts of the movement's radical ideology are so seldom exposed to external scrutiny. Published in academic journals and books aimed at a readership sympathetic to their anti-male perspective, the rhetoric of feminist intellectuals is often starkly at odds with the bland liberal language of "equality" and "choice" with which the movement speaks in public. In 2014, I began compiling a small library of feminist books, most of them by authors who are little recognized outside the academic field of Women's Studies, where the work of advancing feminist theory is carried on. A study of these books reveals that, for more than four decades, feminist authors have consistently condemned the traditional family as oppressive to women. Furthermore, feminists have repeatedly denounced men and heterosexuality, *per se*, advocating lesbianism as the ultimate in "liberation." What follows are a few samples of the rhetoric that typifies this radicalism.

"Patriarchy's chief institution is the family. . . . [T]he family effects control and conformity where political and other authorities are insufficient. As the fundamental instrument and the foundation unit of patriarchal society the family and its roles are prototypical. . . .

"The concept of romantic love affords a means of emotional manipulation which the male is free to exploit, since love is the only circumstance in which the female is (ideologically) pardoned for sexual activity. . . .

"We are not accustomed to associate patriarchy with force. So perfect is its system of socialization, so complete the general assent to its values, so long and so universally has it prevailed in human society, that it scarcely seems to require violent implementation. . . .

"Historically, most patriarchies have institutionalized force through their legal systems. . . .

"Significantly, force itself is restricted to the male who alone is psychologically and technically equipped to perpetrate physical force. . . .

"Patriarchal force also relies on a form of violence particularly sexual in character and realized most completely in the act of rape. The figures of rapes reported represent only a fraction of those which occur. . . ."

— Kate Millett, *Sexual Politics* (1970)

"We want to destroy sexism, that is, polar role definitions of male and female, man and woman. We want to destroy patriarchal power at its source, the family; in its most hideous form, the nation-state. We want to destroy the structure of culture as we know it, its art, its churches, its laws . . .

"We are born into a world in which sexual possibilities are narrowly circumscribed. . . . We are programmed by the culture as surely as rats are programmed to make the arduous way through the scientist's maze, and that programming operates on every level of choice and action."
— Andrea Dworkin, *Woman Hating* (1974)

"That some men rape provides a sufficient threat to keep all women in a constant state of intimidation, forever conscious of the knowledge that the biological tool must be held in awe, for it may turn to weapon with sudden swiftness born of harmful intent. . . . Rather than society's aberrants or 'spoilers of purity,' men who commit rape have served in effect as front-line masculine shock troops, terrorist guerrillas in the longest sustained battle the world has ever known."
— Susan Brownmiller, *Against Our Will: Men, Women, and Rape* (1975)

"I agreed to take part in a New York University Institute for Humanities conference a year ago. . . .

"I stand here as a black lesbian feminist, having been invited to comment within the only panel at this conference where the input of black feminists and lesbians is represented. What this says about the vision of this conference is sad, in a country where racism, sexism and homophobia are inseparable. . . .

"The absence of any consideration of lesbian consciousness or the consciousness of third world women leaves a serious gap within this conference. . . .

"For women, the need and desire to nurture each other is not pathological but redemptive, and it is within that knowledge that our real power is rediscovered. It is this real connection, which is so feared by a patriarchal world."
— Audre Lorde, "The Master's Tools Will Never Dismantle the Master's House," 1979

"I want to ask heterosexual academic feminists to do some hard analytical and reflective work. To begin, I want to say to them:
"I wish you would notice that you are heterosexual.

"I wish you would grow to the understanding that you choose heterosexuality.

"I would like you to rise each morning and know that you are heterosexual and that you choose to be heterosexual — that you are and choose to be a member of a privileged and dominant class, one of your privileges being not to notice.

"I wish you would stop and seriously consider, as a broad and long-term feminist political strategy, the conversion of women to a woman-identified and woman-directed sexuality and eroticism, as a way of breaking the grip of men on women's minds and women's bodies, of removing women from the chronic attachment to the primary situations of sexual and physical violence that is rained upon women by men, and as a way of promoting women's firm and reliable bonding against oppression. . . .

"There is so much pressure on women to be heterosexual, and this pressure is both so pervasive and so completely denied, that I think heterosexuality cannot come naturally to many women: I think that widespread heterosexuality among women is a highly artificial product of the patriarchy. . . . I think that most women have to be coerced into heterosexuality."

— Marilyn Frye, "A Lesbian's Perspective on Women's Studies" (1980)

"A materialist feminist approach to women's oppression destroys the idea that women are a 'natural group' . . . What the analysis accomplishes on the level of ideas, practice makes actual at the level of facts: by its very existence, lesbian society destroys the artificial (social) fact constituting women as a 'natural group.' A lesbian society pragmatically reveals that the division from men of which women have been the object is a political one . . .

"Lesbian is the only concept I know of which is beyond the categories of sex (woman and man). . . . For what makes a woman is a specific social relation to a man, a relation that we have previously called servitude . . . a relation which lesbians escape by refusing to become or to stay heterosexual. . . . [O]ur survival demands that we contribute all our strength to the destruction of the class of women within which men appropriate women. This can be accomplished only by the destruction of heterosexuality as a social system which is based on the oppression of women by men and which produces the doctrine of the difference between the sexes to justify this oppression."

— Monique Wittig, "One Is Not Born a Woman" (1981)

"When we consider the family, we have to talk about child sexual abuse, incest, and the area of family violence that I've focused on: wife abuse, marital rape, and battering — often culminating, in the cases I've looked into, in homicide. . . . Exploring our sexuality requires freedom, and for women the family structure is still a prison. . . .

"Family 'stability' in a patriarchal system depends upon sexual repression of women. . . .

"We know that men beat women because they can. No one stops them because to do so would be to interfere with the family. . . .

"Violence has always been an important tool for maintaining the family to serve the purposes of patriarchy. . . .

"Susan Brownmiller's [1976] book, Against Our Will, is a milestone in the women's movement because it demythologized — desexualized — rape. We learned . . . that sexual and physical violence against women is not 'sexual' at all but simply violent. Men use it to dominate women. . . .

"Susan Brownmiller showed us that the rapists serve all men by enforcing male supremacy. . . . [W]e should be clear that our quarrel is not only with certain abusive men but with male supremacy. Our goal should be not merely to redefine our sexuality but to redefine the world and our place in it."
— Ann Jones, "Family Matters," in *The Sexual Liberals and the Attack on Feminism*, edited by Dorchen Leidholdt and Janice G. Raymond (1990)

"Is there some commonality among 'women' that preexists their oppression, or do 'women' have a bond by virtue of their oppression alone? Is there a specificity to women's cultures that is independent of their subordination by hegemonic, masculinist cultures? . . .

"Is the construction of the category of women as a coherent and stable subject an unwitting regulation and reification precisely contrary to feminist aims? . . . To what extent does the category of women achieve stability and coherence only in the context of the heterosexual matrix?"
— Judith Butler, *Gender Trouble: Feminism and the Subversion of Identity* (1990)

"The professionals who diagnose women's sexual maladjustments never question the politics of these 'problems.' They rarely address fundamental issues such as: Why should women get married? Why should we enjoy 'feminine' clothing?

What is wrong with 'homosexual tendencies'? . . . Indeed, why should women want sex with men at all? . . .

"Radical feminist practice is concerned about recognizing our fear, and anger, and refusing to dismiss those reactions as simply 'dysfunctional.' It is about organizing collectively to challenge the institutions that deny women's rage and pain. It is about questioning 'common-sense' understandings of the world. Radical feminists have examined the institution of heterosexuality, the social construction of desire and the links between rape and 'consensual' sex. These analyses question the existence of 'truly chosen' and 'egalitarian' heterosexual relations by focusing on the compulsory enforcement of heterosexuality; they are suspicious of appeals to some 'authentic female sexuality,' hidden deep within ourselves and uncontaminated by the rule of heteropatriarchy."
— Jenny Kitzinger, "Sexual Violence and Compulsory Heterosexuality," in *Heterosexuality: A Feminism & Psychology Reader*, edited by Sue Wilkinson and Celia Kitzinger (1993)

"[T]he seductiveness of lesbianism for feminism lies in the former's figuration of a female desiring subjectivity to which all women may accede . . [T]he erotic charge of a desire for women . . . unlike male desire, affirms and enhances the female-sexed subject and represents her possibility of access to a sexuality autonomous from the male. . . .

"Some women have 'always' been lesbians. Others, like myself, have 'become' one. As much a sociocultural construction as it is an effect of early childhood experiences, sexual identity is nether innate nor simply acquired, but dynamically (re)structured by forms of fantasy private and public, conscious and unconscious, which are culturally available and historically specific."
— Teresa de Lauretis, *The Practice of Love: Lesbian Sexuality and Perverse Desire* (1994)

"[Charlotte Bunch's 1972 manifesto] 'Lesbians in Revolt' argued one powerful and uncompromising principle: because sexism is the root of all oppression and heterosexuality upholds sexism, feminists must become lesbians and lesbians must become feminists if we are to effect a revolution. . . . To state that feminists must become lesbians assumes that lesbianism is a matter of choice and conviction, not biological conditioning or sexual behavior. Moreover, lesbians must also become feminists, that is, they must ground their sexuality in a political discourse if any social change is to occur. . . .

"Lesbian criticism of any and all varieties was constructed by flesh and bone lesbians starting in the early 1970s. For us, feminism was not a distinct discourse that spoke 'for' lesbians but an epistemology used by lesbians to speak for ourselves. . . . I believe it can be shown that, historically, lesbianism and feminism have been coterminous if not identical social phenomena."

— Bonnie Zimmerman, "Confessions of a Lesbian Feminist," in *Cross Purposes: Lesbians, Feminists, and the Limits of Alliance*, edited by Dana Heller (1997)

"Heterosexuality is a category divided by gender and which also depends for its meaning on gender divisions. . . .

"The view that heterosexuality is a key site of male power is widely accepted within feminism. Within most feminist accounts, heterosexuality is seen not as an individual preference, something we are born like or gradually develop into, but as a socially constructed institution which structures and maintains male domination, in particular through the way it channels women into marriage and motherhood. Similarly, lesbianism has been defined not just as a particular sexual practice, but as a form of political struggle — a challenge to the institution of heterosexuality and a form of resistance to patriarchal relations."

— Dianne Richardson, "Theorizing Heterosexuality," in *Rethinking Sexuality* (2000)

"Far from being 'natural,' phallic sexuality is a moral and political activity. . . . Men's sexual behaviour is not caused by hormonal dictates. It is because the penis serves the ideological function of symbolizing 'human' status that it is so heavily charged with erotic energy, and not because it is driven by testosterone. Men must keep using it because they need to keep proving that they exist, that their 'humanity' is inextricably entwined with penis-possession; women must be constantly used by it to prove that men exist, that the sum total of a man is his penis. . . . Anything and everything must be subordinated to penile activity if men are to be what phallic ideology requires them to be."

— Denise Thompson, *Radical Feminism Today* (2001)

Many of these authors were or are professors at major universities, and some of the works quoted (Brownmiller, Lorde, Wittig and

Butler) are part of the core curriculum of Women's Studies as taught to many thousands of students annually. What emerges from a reading of such feminist works is an ideology profoundly hostile not only to men, but to the basic institutions and practices of what most women would consider a normal, happy life. The feminist movement's goal – "to destroy the structure of culture as we know it," as Dworkin said – is incompatible not merely with marriage and the family, but with the principles of democratic government. In order to obtain the androgynous "equality" that is the objective of feminist ideology, religion freedom will have to be abolished, along with the free speech rights of feminism's critics. Unless we are willing to oppose feminist *now*, we may find ourselves eventually living in a totalitarian society where such opposition is prohibited by law.

Kate Millett's Tedious Madness

"[A] disinterested examination of our system of sexual relationship must point out that the situation between the sexes now, and throughout history, is . . . a relationship of dominance and subordinance. What goes largely unexamined, often even unacknowledged (yet is institutionalized nonetheless) in our social order, is the birthright priority whereby males rule females. . . .

"This is so because our society, like all other historical civilizations, is a patriarchy."
— Kate Millett, *Sexual Politics* (1970)

KATE MILLETT IS A GOOD PROSE STYLIST and also a sadistic perverted psychopath. On the latter subject, I will accept the testimony of Millett's younger sister, Mallory Millett:

> In the 1970's I was alarmed to hear that my big sister, Kate Millett, who had serious mental health issues which had agonized my family and her friends for many years, was organizing a group called The Mental Patients' Project in order to claim that the psychiatric community and society were "oppressing" people and "stigmatizing them with labels such as psychotic, bi-polar, schizophrenic, borderline personalities," etc and unconstitutionally imprisoning them in hospitals thereby violating their civil rights. We, as a family, had struggled for years with Kate's issues, many times attempting to hospitalize her so she could obtain the serious help she so obviously obviously needed. She was a brutal sadist, a violent bully at whose hands everyone about her suffered. Throughout my childhood I was menaced and immeasurably traumatized . . .
>
> At one point, in 1973, I found myself alone with her in an apartment in Berkeley, California where she did not allow me to sleep for five days as she raged at the world and menaced me physically. . . .
>
> And, speaking of the affected innocent victims: later, she wrote a book about her lesbian lover at that time. *Sita* was the title. This woman committed suicide in response to Kate's "homage." . .

.

Although I had known that Kate Millett was a bisexual weirdo, it was not until somebody called my attention to this firsthand account by her sister that I realized what a certified raving lunatic she was.

Psychosis and feminism are, often enough, two words that describe the same phenomenon. Shulamith Firestone was a paranoid schizophrenic, Women's Studies professor Lisa Johnson is afflicted with borderline personality disorder, and if I had a nickel for every feminist who had ever lamented her "struggle" with chronic depression, I'd certainly have more than the price of a carton of cigarettes.

The difference between mental illness and feminist theory is . . . *nuanced.* Was anyone surprised when the eminent "male feminist," Professor Hugo Schwarz, was revealed to be dangerous psychotic? It is difficult to avoid the suspicion that Women's Studies majors are all demented freaks who, if they couldn't afford to go to college, would be in psychiatric hospitals, where their deranged babbling about "gender roles," "patriarchy" and "heteronormativity" would earn them a daily dose of Thorazine, rather than a Bachelor of Arts degree.

Despite her mental illness, however, Kate Millett writes good prose, and I think this is a factor that should not be overlooked. Like many another high-functioning psychotic, Millett is intelligent. She once taught English at the college level, and *Sexual Politics* was an adaptation of her Ph.D. dissertation at Columbia University. Smart and well-educated, Millett published *Sexual Politics* when she was 36. Her prose has a mature quality that is absent in Firestone's zany *The Dialectic of Sex,* published when Firestone was 22.

Millett begins her book with a clever trick: She excerpts and subjects to literary criticism sex scenes from three novels — Henry Miller's *Sexus* (1965), Norman Mailer's *An American Dream* (1964) and Jean Genet's *The Thief's Journal* (1964) — by authors who were then fashionable. Henry Miller's writing was so pornographic that his books were often banned in the U.S. prior to the 1960s; *Sexus* was published in Paris in 1949 and not published in the U.S. until 16 years later. Norman Mailer, of course, soared to fame when his first novel, *The Naked and the Dead,* became a bestseller in 1948, when he was just 25. He never quite replicated that success in fiction; although his subsequent novels sold well, they were less critically acclaimed, and Mailer's reputation as a writer was mostly based on his works of journalism and non-fiction. He won the Pulitzer Prize for *The Armies of the Night,* his non-fiction account of a 1967 anti-war march, and his 1980 Pulitzer winner *The Executioner's Song,* was about the life of murderer Gary Gilmore. As for Jean Genet, he was a notorious French degenerate who gained fame after Jean-Paul Sartre made him the subject of a 1952 book, *Saint Genet.*

The scene Millett quotes from Miller's *Sexus* involves the protagonist sexually assaulting the wife of his friend. The scene she quotes from Mailer involves a murderer sodomizing his German maid. The scene she quotes from Genet involves a transvestite prostitute and his/her pimp.

In each case, Millett highlights through her criticism the aspect of *power* — male supremacy — in the sexual context. These "notions of power and ascendancy," Millett says, demonstrate that sex does not "take place in a vacuum," but rather is "a charged microcosm of the variety of attitudes and values to which culture subscribes." This is both true and highly problematic. Obviously, it is true that our attitudes and behaviors about sex are influenced by culture. But where Millett is headed with this argument — the purpose of her nearly 400-page book — is toward the claim that there are no meaningful *natural* differences between men and women, that the associations male/masculine and female/feminine are *artificial*, and that anything which can be labeled "male supremacy" is therefore inherently *political* in nature.

Let it not be said that Millett was unable to marshal any evidence on behalf of her argument. Anyone may order *Sexual Politics* from Amazon and examine her argument and her evidence. The problems with Millett's book arise mainly from three causes:

1. **Her fundamentally anti-social attitude.** Millett's purposes are admittedly revolutionary. She aims to destroy the existing society, and all its patriarchal "values and attitudes," without any regard for the personal happiness of anyone who is content with life in this society, having successfully adapted to "our system of sexual relationship." This contempt for the lives of other people is characteristic of a sociopathic personality. Her sister's revelation of Kate Millett's domineering and sadistic behaviors are quite relevant to our understanding of Millett's motivations.

2. **Her tendentious selectivity of evidence**. Of course, every radical argument suffers from this flaw. If your aim is to overthrow The System in a democratic polity where electoral governance and the Rule of Law have the effect of continually ratifying The System, your argument for revolution must necessarily be based on unusual evidence. You must ignore, or subject to scorn and ridicule as "reactionary," every argument made by defenders of The System. Despite her early acknowledgement (page 25) that a patriarchal social order was characteristic not just of America in 1970, but of "all other historical civilizations," Millett deliberately rejects all evidence that such a social order is natural or inevitable.

3. **Her substitution of rhetorical gestures for actual logic**. As I say, Millett's prose is quite good and, like many intellectuals, she seems to believe that her ability to express an argument in stylish prose is proof that her argument must be true. The fact that other

intellectuals, equally articulate, hold opposing views, is a problem Millett evades by accusing her antagonists of prejudice. Her fluency in exposition is, for Millett, a camouflage used to conceal extraordinary leaps of logic. She asserts a startling premise, based on evidence that is negligible or controversial or at least unusual, and then continues her argument as if the premise were a proven fact. One finds, for example, that Millett spends 19 pages (108-127) discussing Friedrich Engels' *The Origin of the Family, Private Property and the State* (1884), and finds nothing amiss with treating the co-author of *The Communist Manifesto* as an objective analyst. When Engels' name recurs on page 169, it is in the context of Millett's analysis of the failure of the Bolsheviks' attempt to abolish the family in the Soviet Union. Millett cites the criticism of Leon Trotsky as an authority on "the Stalinist regression" in this matter, without bothering to explain why Trotsky might have blamed this failure on Stalin personally, rather than on the hopeless impracticality of the Bolshevik ideal.

Also, generally, *Sexual Politics* is boring. Her hammering of the same points becomes repetitive to the point of tedium.

Nature, Nuture and Feminist Theory

Any well-educated reader hostile to Millett's basic claims can read *Sexual Politics* and compose his own point-by-point refutation. It would be interesting to see some graduate student in psychology or anthropology make such a critical project the subject of a master's thesis or doctoral dissertation. However, one supposes that any aspiring scholar capable of such a project is smart enough to know that doing this work would be the kiss of death to his career in academia. Nor would I, as a shameless capitalist, devote myself to that project; there is no market demand for such a point-by-point rebuttal, and I would not bother my readers with that kind endless tedium, merely to prove myself capable of producing a rebuttal to the arguments of an articulate psychotic with a Ph.D.

Nevertheless, because readers of my blog have generously contributed to fund my in-depth investigation of radical feminism, let me briefly point out some obvious examples of Millett's sophistry. On page 30 of *Sexual Politics*, she writes:

Psychosexually (*e.g.*, in terms of masculine and feminine, and in contradistinction to male and female) there is no differentiation between the sexes at birth. Psychosexual personality is therefore postnatal and learned.

This was written in 1970, just past the peak of Freudian prestige, when scientific claims of human differences based in genetic heredity ("nature") were in disrepute, and when those who attributed human differences to the influences of early family life and societal expectations ("nurture") were at the apogee of their ascendancy in academia, in law and in popular culture.

Millett certainly was not the only intellectual of her era who subscribed to the developmental concept of human personality, a perspective which was at that time hegemonic in its dominance of every elite institution, from the college campus to the psychoanalyst's couch to the Supreme Court. Advances in our understanding of genetics, in prenatal development and the influence of hormones on the brain, have refuted much of what was believed by elite intellectuals circa 1970 in terms of "psychosexual personality." The insights from research have given rise to speculation based on evolutionary theory.

Scientific advances have been quite unfortunate for Millett's claim that "there is no differentiation between the sexes at birth," in part because her citation for that claim is dependent on one of the greatest frauds in scientific history. On pages 30-31, she excerpts a quotation from a 1965 article "Psychosexual Differentation," from a book entitled *Sex Research, New Developments*; in her bibliography, Millett references a 1957 book, *The Psychologic Study of Man*. The author of both of these works was Johns Hopkins University psychologist Dr. John Money, whose botched attempt to turn a boy into a girl (the notorious "John/Joan" experiment) failed spectacularly, ultimately resulting in the suicide of Dr. Money's pathetic human guinea pig, David Reimer.

Dr. Money's unethical (and perhaps criminal) methods of attempting to psychologically "condition" Reimer to be a girl were never successful; "Brenda" Reimer aggressively rejected the female identity that Dr. Money tried to impose. Yet Dr. Money, having trumpeted the "John/Joan" case as proof of his theories in the 1970s, misrepresented the case in his academic publications and in popular media. It took many years before another scientist, curious to know how Dr. Money's patient had adjusted to adult womanhood, discovered the shocking truth behind Dr. Money's fraudulent "research." As a teenager, "Brenda" Reimer had decisively rejected "her" female identity, and sought treatment to become the man "she" had been born to be. David Reimer married a woman and, despite the loss of functional genitalia — castrated in infancy as part of Dr. Money's "treatment" — he was by the 1990s an otherwise normal (that is, *masculine*) young man, albeit suffering from depression that finally resulted in his 2004 suicide.

Grant that Kate Millett had no way of knowing, in 1970, that Dr. Money's theories were already being proven false in practice, because of Dr. Money's dishonesty about the results. Still, his theories were always controversial, and his critics (including Dr. Milton Diamond, who eventually exposed the fraud) were not silent. Yet these critics were ignored by Millett, and scientists whose findings did not comport with Millett's ideology — we must view her as a pioneer of what feminists today call "gender theory" — were subjected to dismissive ridicule. From page 32 of *Sexual Politics*:

> Here it might be added . . . that data from physical sciences has recently been enlisted again to support sociological arguments, such as those of Lionel Tiger who seeks a genetic justification of patriarchy by proposing a "bonding instinct" in males which assures their political and social control of human society. . . .Tiger's thesis appears to be a misrepresentation of the work of [Konrad] Lorenz and other students of animal behavior. Since [Tiger's] evidence of inherent trait is patriarchal history and organization, his pretensions to physical evidence are both specious and circular.

Any student of behavioral science will probably be as shocked by this passage as I am, as a student of rhetoric. Millett, whose claim to expertise was . . . well, *what?* She got her bachelor's degree in English from the University of Minnesota and got a postgraduate degree in literature at Oxford University, then went to Japan where she taught English and married an avant-garde sculptor.

Here she was in 1970, however, presuming to accuse Dr. Lionel Tiger, a professor of anthropology, of misrepresenting the research of zoologist Konrad Lorenz, who won the Nobel Prize in 1973. If Tiger was guilty of misrepresenting Lorenz's work, you might think that Lorenz himself would have made the accusation, which he never did. Anyone interested in the subject may consult Konrad Lorenz's 1966 book *On Aggression* and Lionel Tiger's 1968 book *Men in Groups* and decide for themselves whether the two authors were in accord. The reader may also consult Harvard biologist E.O. Wilson's 1978 book *On Human Nature* (for which Professor Wilson was awarded the Pulitzer Prize) wherein he offers a learned examination of Lorenz's theories. As Professor Tiger and Professor Wilson are in substantial agreement about evolution and human behavior, I'm willing to bet that both of them agree that what Lorenz said about aggression in animals has relevance to "bonding instinct" in human males. Yet we see how Millett, who was willing to accept Dr. John Money's strange theories of gender without question, arrogated to herself the authority to disregard Professor Tiger's research, accusing him of "misrepresentation" of another scientist's work, and dismissing Professor Tiger's claim to scientific knowledge as "pretension . . . both specious and circular."

'Science Falsely So Called'

Far be it from me, of course, to appoint myself as Official Referee of any dispute between zoologists, anthropologists and other specialists in scientific fields relevant to human behavior. As a Bible-believing

Christian, I am profoundly skeptical that any research based on Darwinian theory can tell us much about the true origins of such phenomena. It is interesting to me to see what we actually know about human behavior, and interesting to see how scientists try to explain this as theory based on Darwinian concepts. However, I can never cede the fundamental claim of Darwinism, *i.e.*, that all of this is a random accident of the universe, and that we are all therefore "evolved" from some bit of primordial slime. Always, I keep in mind the Apostle Paul's warning to Timothy about "profane and vain babblings, and oppositions of science falsely so called." This warning applies equally to Darwinian anthropology as to feminism, neither of which is the basis of my own belief system. But I digress . . .

Kate Millett's cunning sophistry is such that, if anyone is predisposed in her favor — a disgruntled woman eager for an articulate assault on male prerogative — it is an easy thing to overlook her clever tricks of rhetoric. Over and over in the pages of *The Politics of Sex*, Millett asserts a premise, offers dubious or controversial evidence in support of her premise, pretends to discredit all claims to the contrary, and then proceeds to make her (unproven) premise the basis of further argument. She does this with great skill, so that you wouldn't notice it unless by force of habit you had learned to look for such tricks. A forensic examination of *The Politics of Sex* could, as I say, provide a thesis or dissertation for the graduate student willing to undertake such a project.

Consider, for example, how she accuses Professor Tiger of seeking "a genetic *justification* of patriarchy," as if the anthropologist were advocating or defending a particular system of behavior, rather than offering an analytical theory. Millett used the tendentious word "justification" when "explanation" would have been more appropriate, and *The Politics of Sex* is crammed full of such tricks. Having insinuated that Professor Tiger's theories are misguided and deceptive, see where Millett then proceeds on page 32:

One can only advance genetic evidence when one has genetic (rather than historical) evidence to advance. As many authorities dismiss the possibility of instincts (complex inherent behavior patterns) in humans altogether, admitting only reflexes and drives (far simpler neural responses), the prospects of a 'bonding instinct" appear particularly forlorn.

Kate Millett argues science with all the skill typical of an English major. Note how she invokes "many authorities" to lull readers into accepting the distinction between human instincts (*impossible!*) and mere "reflexes and drives," so Professor Tiger's theory about an instinctive basis of male bonding can be dismissed as a "forlorn" prospect. Millet does not inform her readers, of course, that Professor Tiger's theories of male bonding were based on *direct observation of actual human behavior*, across many cultures, so that what he was attempting to explain (not "justify," as Millett would have us think) was a phenomenon so universal it would be difficult to imagine how it could have a *non*-genetic basis. And look how Millett then continues her argument:

> Should one regard sex in humans as a drive, it is still necessary to point out that the enormous area of our lives, both in early "socialization" and in adult experience, labeled "sexual behavior," is almost entirely the product of learning. So much is this the case that even the act of coitus itself is the product of a long series of learned responses — responses to the patterns and attitudes, even as to the object of sexual choice, which are set up for us by our social environment.
>
> The arbitrary ascription of temperament and role has little effect upon their power over us. Nor do the mutually exclusive, contradictory, and polar qualities of the categories "masculine" and "feminine" imposed upon human personality give rise to sufficiently serious question among us. Under their aegis each personality becomes little more, and often less than half, of its human potential.

At this point, any honest, intelligent and reasonably well-informed person reading *The Politics of Sex* must be tempted to fling the book into the nearest garbage can. Common sense tells us that, without regard to whether sex is a "drive" or a matter of "learned responses," sexual intercourse between man and woman is necessary to the survival of the species. Insofar as human beings procreate successfully, we must suppose that this behavior is in some way hard-wired into minds and bodies. Only the most fanatical ideologue could look around our planet, where there are now more than *7 billion* human beings, and claim that this has nothing to do with "sex in humans as a drive" — but this sort of ideological fanaticism is the driving force of Kate Millett's feminism.

Likewise, anyone may look at actual men and women (rather than mere *theories* about them) and ask whether "the categories 'masculine' and 'feminine' [are] *imposed* upon human personality," as Millett claims, or whether these words are simply a common-sense description of men and women as they exist in real life. Grant that some men are more masculine than others, acknowledge there are effeminate men and "mannish" women — these are variations that no one denies, and which in no way contradict anything in our common-sense understanding of masculinity and femininity. Yet for Millett, these things become the theoretical foundation upon which she erects a vast superstructure of argument on behalf of feminist revolution. Here is how she concludes on page 363:

> When one surveys the spontaneous mass movements taking place all over the world, one is led to hope that human understanding itself has grown ripe for change. In America one may expect the

new women's movement to ally itself on an equal basis with blacks and students in a growing radical coalition. It is also possible that women now represent a very crucial element capable of swinging the national mood, poised at this moment between the alternatives of progress and political repression, toward meaningful change. As the largest alienated element in our society, and because of their numbers, passion, and length of oppression, its largest revolutionary base, women might come to play a leadership in social revolution, quite unknown before in history. The changes in fundamental values such a coalition of expropriated groups — blacks, youth, women, the poor — would seek are especially pertinent to realizing not only sexual revolution but a gathering impetus toward freedom from rank or prescriptive role, sexual or otherwise. For to actually change the quality of life is to transform personality, and this cannot be done without freeing humanity from tyranny of sexual-social category and conformity to sexual stereotype — as well as abolishing racial caste and economic class.

Kate Millett was obviously not a woman with small ambitions. To envision women as the "largest revolutionary base" leading "a coalition of expropriated groups" on behalf of "social revolution" — well, you'd have to be *insane* to imagine such a thing, and within a few years, Kate Millett's insanity was obvious to everyone. Her sister Mallory describes Kate's public breakdown in 1973:

During the speech [at the University of California-Berkeley] after the screening [of the Millett's feminist documentary film Three Lives] she fell apart onstage before a packed assembly of fawning admirers. It was a standing room only audience. In fact, they had had to schedule a second screening at the last minute, as the response had been huge. As I sat next to her lectern during her incoherent ravings I witnessed the pained looks of confusion as they swept across those faces like a small gale whipping up across the top of a sea; at first tiny ripples gliding across the surface. They were polite until the realization took shape that she was making no sense whatsoever. People began glancing at each other, whispering a little then turning to one another with more energy, politeness gone, as some began to get up and leave. Soon many were slipping out and that was followed by a mad dash for the exits. She was babbling and shouting incoherently whilst I nodded and pretended every word made perfect sense. I could not bear to betray her in public. I sat there feeling my heart melting through my chest and draining into my belly with an indescribable sick empathy. Her humiliation was unbearable as the gale whipped up to a force ten and with one last enormous surge we were left in an empty room. The second screening was cancelled.

What ensued for Mallory Millett was a five-day nightmare trapped with her famous sister, who was in the grip of a psychotic rage:

> Unable to abandon her, I stayed and whenever possible reached out by phone to other family members/friends in far flung places such as NYC, Minnesota, Nebraska pleading for advice and help. One such conversation was with Yoko Ono, a good friend of hers, who called to check on Kate and from whom I tearfully begged advice. . . .
>
> Our elder sister, Sally, eventually came from Nebraska to the rescue, as it was imperative I return to NY to join a European theatrical tour for which I was contracted. She managed to get some temporary care for Kate, which sufficed for the moment. Within time, our mother and a lawyer nephew managed to take Kate to court in Minnesota in order to secure her "commitment." Anyone who knows Kate Millett knows the depth of her shrewdness which she used to bring in a NY lawyer and, in her unglued state, she stood up for herself as only she can and to our great horror prevailed in that courtroom walking out, unrestrained, to spend many more years, lurching about the world to continue her damaging and irrational antics; her genius for chaos. Subsequently, she boarded a plane for Shannon, Ireland and upon arrival locked herself in the Ladies Room preventing anyone from relieving herself for twenty-four hours until the Shannon police broke down the door and committed her to an Irish psychiatric institution. She got word out to some of her Irish feminist loyalists who smuggled her out through a window and she escaped to be on the run making her way back to NYC. Many of her friends in the US were now involved and other interventions were arranged which she also managed to elude, quoting The Constitution to police and ambulance drivers.

Keep in mind that all this transpired just three years after Kate Millett was feted on the cover of *Time* magazine. Perhaps her feminist admirers could tell themselves that all Millett's problems were the fault of the oppressive patriarchy, but doesn't it seem that at least some of them should have experienced second thoughts about their movement? When one of the foremost leaders of your "social revolution" is revealed to be a raving lunatic, doesn't this call into question the theories she had previously proclaimed? Alas, it was the '70s, when people didn't feel ridiculous wearing polyester bell-bottoms and some people even thought it would be a good idea to nominate George McGovern for president. The '70s were the Golden Age of Bad Ideas, the era of the Symbionese Liberation Army, the Ford Pinto and the Jonestown Massacre. Unlike other fads and disasters of the '70s, however, feminism endures.

The strange persistence of feminism's bad ideas can be explained simply enough. Unlike the Jim Jones cult that died in the jungles of Guyana, the feminist cult institutionalized itself, building a permanent base of operations in the Women's Studies departments of universities and colleges. Every year, many tens of thousands of naive young women are indoctrinated in feminist ideology through these programs, and the influence of their bad ideas has been extended into every academic discipline — particularly history, psychology and law — so that now, after many decades, feminist ideas are accepted without question on campus. This institutionalization of feminism has the effect of creating a market demand for feminist books, as well as a career track for would-be professors of Women's Studies. Furthermore, as feminist influence has entrenched itself in higher education, it has acquired a terrifying power to intimidate its critics within academia. The voice of feminism's critics is seldom heard on American campuses today.

'Sexual Politics,' Secrets and Insanity

Strange to say, however, in the early 1990s, the publishers of Kate Millett's pioneering book *Sexual Politics* let it go out of print. As Millett recounts in the preface to the 2000 edition, it took nearly seven years and numerous rejections from publishers before the University of Illinois Press offered to re-publish it. Why was this so? Well, despite her radicalism, Millett's views on certain subjects had become somewhat obsolete. In the late 1980s and early '90s, militant lesbians like Michigan State University Professor Marilyn Frye began to insist that Women's Studies programs cease their embarrassed silence about lesbianism. Avant-garde exponents of "gender theory" like Professor Judith Butler, herself an unapologetic lesbian, emerged as the voices of so-called "Third Wave" feminism, and what did Kate Millett have to say about all that? A single footnote on pp. 336-337 of *Sexual Politics*:

> Following custom, the term 'homosexual' refers to male
> homosexuals here. "Lesbianism" would appear to be so little
> threat at the moment that it is hardly ever mentioned. . . .
> Whatever its potentiality in sexual politics, female homosexuality
> is currently so dead an issue that while male homosexuality gains
> a grudging tolerance, in women the event is observed in scorn or
> silence.

Oops. Millett's hypocrisy about lesbian "potentiality" was a cause of immediate grief after her book was published in 1970. She was married to a man, but had engaged in lesbian affairs, and many radical "sisters" in the Women's Liberation movement knew it. During an event at Columbia University in November 1970, just three months after she had appeared on the cover of *Time*, Millett was participating in a panel discussion onstage when the heckling began. Feminist historian Susan Brownmiller described the confrontation:

> Minutes into the panel a voice from the back of the hall rang out, "Bisexuality is a cop-out!"
>
> Sidney Abbott, another panel member, peered into the audience and recognized Ann Sanchez, one of the Radicalesbians.
>
> The persistent voice catcalled, "Are you a lesbian, Kate? What are you afraid of? You say it downtown, but you don't say it uptown. Why won't you say it?"
>
> "Yes," Millett wearily replied. "You think bisexuality is a cop-out, so yes, I'll say it. I am a lesbian."
>
> A reporter from *Time* was at her door the next morning. The story ran in December. Millett's disclosure of her bisexuality, the magazine intoned, avoiding the word "lesbian," was "bound to discredit her as a spokeswoman for the cause."
>
> Dolores Alexander and Ivy Bottini of [the National Organization for Women] urgently called a "Kate Is Great" press conference. Artemis March and Ellen Shumsky of the Radicalesbians composed a statement of solidarity that was read to the reporters. . . . Gloria Steinem firmly held Kate's hand for a significant photo for the *Times*. . . But the show of support did little to calm the fraying nerves of the woman who stood at center of the media storm. . . .
>
> *Sexual Politics* would never be dislodged from its place as feminism's first book-length bombshell, but the making and breaking of Kate Millett as the movement's high priestess had run its course in four months.

The destruction of Kate Millett's "high priestess" status is significant in several ways, most importantly as a foreshadowing of feminism's future direction. It wasn't the sexist patriarchy that destroyed her, it was radical lesbians who refused to let Millett get away with dishonest two-faced hypocrisy about her own sexuality.

"The personal is political," after all.

Yet for decades to come, and still to this day in many cases, feminism continues to engage in the same kind of hypocrisy that unraveled so quickly for Kate Millett in 1970. It is scarcely a secret within academia that Women's Studies programs are now dominated by lesbian faculty using textbooks that prominently feature lesbian authors.

What this signifies should be obvious: Feminist theory is ultimately incompatible with the normal lives of normal women who, whatever their career ambitions or political beliefs, hope to find happiness in a life that involves   men,   marriage   and   motherhood.

Yet the pioneers of the feminist movement — women like Shulamith Firestone and Kate Millett — didn't live such lives, and the intellectuals who have followed in the footsteps of those early radicals of Women's Liberation are not living such lives either. Judith Butler and "Queer Theory" are now the hot topics in Women's Studies classes, and the biggest arguments within feminism involve transsexualism and so-called "butch/femme" roles in lesbian culture. Cutting edge feminist research nowadays involves such topics as whether Disney cartoons are imposing heterosexual identity on unsuspecting young girls. (*The Little Mermaid?* Yep — it's patriarchal propaganda.)

Feminists get angry when critics call attention to evidence that Women's Studies programs are now "Lesbo Recruitment 101" — even when you're quoting an employee of the Feminist Majority Foundation on the subject. The two-faced hypocrisy continues and we must ask, what are the consequences of such dishonesty?

Whatever was actually true in Millett's arguments should be accepted as self-evident at this point, more than four decades after her book became the much-heralded manifesto of Women's Liberation, blazoned on the cover of *Time* magazine. Yet here we are, with women more "liberated" (and more equal) in America than at any time or place in the history of the world, and we find that feminism is still controversial. If the iniquities of patriarchal society circa 1970 have been in some measure abolished or eroded, feminists continue to complain about patriarchy as if nothing had changed, and we may well ask if many of the grievances that feminists complain about now are not, in fact, the consequences of previous "reforms" that feminists demanded. Feminists now stage protests dressed in pink vagina costumes and march in SlutWalk demonstrations against "rape culture," and never seem to bother questioning the basic premises of their arguments, much less re-thinking the logic of the arguments based on those premises.

"Truth is great and will prevail," Thomas Jefferson famously observed, and we might wonder how Kate Millett's life and career would have turned out if she hadn't tried to hide the truth about herself in *Sexual Politics*. Her only mention of lesbianism was a single dismissive footnote near the end of the book. What would have been the consequences if, instead of trying to get away with this deception, she had been up-front about her lesbianism? Maybe her book never would have been published, but maybe she wouldn't have gone insane after her dishonesty was exposed. Or maybe — just maybe — Kate Millett was always crazy.

The Indecent Mind of Andrea Dworkin

"Intercourse occurs in a context of a power relation that is pervasive and incontrovertible. The context ... is one in which men have social, economic, political power over women. Some men do not have all those kinds of power over all women; but all men have some kinds of power over all women; and most men have controlling power over what they call *their* women — the women they fuck. The power is predetermined by gender, by being male. ...

"They force us to be compliant, turn us into parasites, then hate us for not letting go. Intercourse is frequently how we hold on: fuck me."

— Andrea Dworkin, *Intercourse* (1987)

HER DEATH IN 2005 REMOVED Andrea Dworkin's strident voice from the angry feminist chorus. She was 58 and died of heart failure, having lived the previous several years in declining health, her knees wrecked by arthritis caused by her morbid obesity. Dworkin fought many battles — and was mostly defeated — during her three-decade career as a feminist scourge. Most notably, during the 1980s, she and fellow radical Catharine MacKinnon tried to pass anti-pornography laws in Minneapolis and Indianapolis. The mayor of Minneapolis vetoed the Dworkin/MacKinnon law there; federal courts ruled the Indianapolis law unconstitutional. Thus, the radicals were defeated by so-called "pro-sex feminists" in their Reagan-era showdown, with consequences that reverberate to the present day.

Andrea Dworkin was a strange and tragic figure. She was abused as a child and abused as an adult, too. In the 1960s, she traveled to Europe, where she engaged in prostitution, "had a passionate romance with a Greek man" and married a Dutch anarchist "who beat the living shit out of her," to quote Ariel Levy's foreword to the 20th anniversary edition of Dworkin's most notorious book, *Intercourse*.

Dworkin was 28 when she published her first feminist book, *Woman Hating: A Radical Look at Sexuality*, in 1974. It is perhaps unnecessary to say that this book suffers from the usual faults of early radical-feminist writing. *Woman Hating* shares with Shulamith Firestone's *The Dialectic of Sex* a utopian vision of what can only be called a post-biological future. Dworkin begins *Woman Hating* thus:

> This book is an action, a political action where revolution is the goal. It has no other purpose. It is not cerebral wisdom, or academic horseshit, or ideas carved in granite or destined for immortality. It is part of a process and its context is change. It is part of a planetary movement to restructure community forms and human consciousness so that people have power over their own lives, participate fully in community, live in dignity and freedom.
> The commitment to ending male dominance as the fundamental psychological, political, and cultural real-ity of earth-lived life is the fundamental revolutionary commitment. It is a commitment to transformation of the self and transformation of the social reality on every level.

Hers is no modest ambition. By the concluding chapter, Dworkin avows herself an apostle of "natural androgynous eroticism":
> The discovery is, of course, that "man" and "woman" are fictions, caricatures, cultural constructs. As models they are reductive, totalitarian, inappropriate to human becoming. As roles they are static, demeaning to the female, dead-ended for male and female both. . . .
> I have defined heterosexuality as the ritualized behavior built on polar role definition. Intercourse with men as we know them is increasingly impossible. It requires an aborting of creativity and strength, a refusal of responsibility and freedom: a bitter personal death. It means remaining the victim, forever annihilating all self-respect. It means acting out the female role, incorporating the masochism, self-hatred, and passivity which are central to

it. Unambiguous conventional heterosexual behavior is the
worst betrayal of our common humanity. . . .

If "conventional heterosexual behavior" is such a "betrayal," then it
logically follows that Dworkin must attack the system of morality
which prohibits not only homosexuality, but other perversions:

The incest taboo does the worst work of the culture: it
teaches us the mechanisms of repressing and internalizing
erotic feeling — it forces us to develop those mechanisms
in the first place; it forces us to particularize sexual feeling,
so that it congeals into a need for a particular sexual
"object"; it demands that we place the nuclear family above
the human family. The destruction of the incest taboo is
essential to the development of cooperative human
community based on the free-flow of natural androgynous
eroticism. . . .

The incest taboo can be destroyed only by destroying the
nuclear family as the primary institution of the culture. The
nuclear family is the school of values in a sexist, sexually
repressed society. One learns what one must know: the
roles, rituals, and behaviors appropriate to male-female
polarity and the internalized mechanisms of sexual
repression. The alternative to the nuclear family at the
moment is the extended family, or tribe. The growth of tribe
is part of the process of destroying particularized roles and
fixed erotic identity. As people develop fluid androgynous
identity, they will also develop the forms of community
appropriate to it. We cannot really imagine what those
forms will be. . . .

Is this true? Are we unable to imagine the forms of "community"
that will emerge if we destroy normal roles associated with the
nuclear family? And are we surprised that, having demanded the
abolition of the incest taboo, that Dworkin advocated the
sexualization of children?

As for children, they too are erotic beings, closer to
androgyny than the adults who oppress them. Children are
fully capable of participating in community, and have every
right to live out their own erotic impulses. In androgynous
community, those impulses would retain a high degree of
nonspecificity and would no doubt show the rest of us the
way into sexual self-realization. The distinctions between

"children" and "adults," and the social institutions which enforce those distinctions, would disappear as androgynous community develops.

You might think anyone who wrote that would be locked up in a psychiatric institution. If not, at least you would suppose that the author of this 1974 book would be regarded as having completely discredited herself by proclaiming such a creepy anti-social vision. To advocate the abolition of the incest taboo (!) and declare that children "have every right to live out their own erotic impulses" (!!) would seem to give *carte blanche* to child molesters, yet this perverse aspect of Dworkin's ideology usually gets overlooked whenever feminists eulogize her. Having written this dangerous 1974 book, which we might expect would have placed her permanently outside the circle of respectability, we find that a dozen years later, Dworkin was under contract to the most respectable of publishers, Simon & Shuster. Feminism created a demand for radical lunacy, and Dworkin was a marketable commodity.

Feminist History: Witches Good, Christians Bad

HOW WAS IT, we may ask, that the wacky (and arguably evil) content of Dworkin's *Woman Hating* did not destroy her career? She probably rescued herself with Chapter 7, "Gynocide: The Witches," a vicious 32-page attack on medieval Christianity. This chapter depicts medieval witches as pagan proto-feminists persecuted by religious patriarchy. These claims have since been debunked by legitimate historians, including the British professor Ronald Hutton, whose 1999 book *The Triumph of the Moon* is arguably the definitive history of modern witchcraft. To give the reader just a taste of what Dworkin wrote in Chapter 7 of *Woman Hating*, try this:

> The origins of the magical content of the pagan cults can be
> traced back to the fairies, who were a real, neolithic people,
> smaller in stature than the natives of northern Europe or
> England. They were a pastoral people who had no
> knowledge of agriculture. They fled before stronger,
> technologically more advanced murderers and missionaries
> who had contempt for their culture. They set up
> communities in the in-lands and concealed their dwellings
> in mounds half hidden in the ground. The fairies developed

those magical skills for which the witches, centuries later, were burned.

The socioreligious organization of the fairy culture was matriarchal and probably polyandrous. The fairy culture was still extant in England as late as the 17th century when even the pagan beliefs of the early witches had degenerated into the Christian parody which we associate with Satanism.

So, here we have fairies not as mythical beings, but as "a real, neolithic people" whose society "was matriarchal and probably polyandrous." Maybe I missed that lecture in my history and anthropology courses. But please continue, Ms. Dworkin:

There was communication between the fairies and the pagan women, and any evidence that a woman had visited the fairies was considered sure proof that she was a witch. There were, then, three separate, though interrelated, phenomena: the fairy race with its matriarchal social organization, its knowledge of esoteric magic and medicine; the woman-oriented fertility cults, also practitioners of esoteric magic and medicine; and later, the diluted witchcraft cults, degenerate parodies of Christianity. There is particular confusion when one tries to distinguish between the last two phenomena. Many of the women condemned by the Inquisition were true devotees of the Old Religion.

Dworkin asserts this as *history*, you see — "communication between the fairies and the pagan women . . . woman-oriented fertility cults . . . esoteric magic and medicine" — and all of this assertion is leading up to a damning accusation several pages later:

We now know most of what can be known about the witches: who they were, what they believed, what they did, the Church's vision of them. We have seen the historical dimensions of a myth of feminine evil which resulted in the slaughter of 9 million persons, nearly all women, over 300 years. The actual evidence of that slaughter, the remembrance of it, has been suppressed for centuries so that the myth of woman as the Original Criminal, the gaping, insatiable womb, could endure. Annihilated with the 9 million was a whole culture, woman-centered, nature-

centered — all of their knowledge is gone, all of their
knowing is destroyed.

This is an astonishing claim: Nine million women were killed in a
span of three centuries, victims of "a myth of feminine evil." Do the
math, and you find that Dworkin is claiming that 30,000 women
were executed for witchcraft every year during the Middle Ages.
Eighty witches killed every day for 300 years, Dworkin wants us to
believe, and all of this witch-killing — the annihilation of "a whole
culture, woman-centered, nature-centered" — she blames on the
Christian church.

Her anti-Christian "history," we may suppose, was enough to
redeem all Dworkin's faults, in the eyes of liberals. What Dworkin
was doing, you see, was a direct reversal of moral values. If you can
accept one such reversal — "Witches *good*, Christians *bad*" — then
it's easier to accept another reversal: "Androgyny *good*, nuclear
family *bad*." And if all this moral reversal leads you to accept
strange ideas like the abolition of incest taboos and children as
"erotic beings"? How convenient!

If your "fundamental revolutionary commitment" is targeted at
"ending male dominance" — and Dworkin could assume her
feminist readers shared that radical commitment — you may be
prepared to accept all manner of weird arguments for the sake of
your goal.

"Thou shalt not suffer a witch to live."
— Exodus 22:18 (KJV)

WHENEVER WE HEAR FEMINISTS CONDEMN "patriarchy," we
understand that what they have in mind is not some kind of
humanitarian democratic reform project. What feminists mean when
they speak of patriarchy is to assert that our entire society and
culture are part of a systemic oppression of women. Four decades
have not changed the ideology of feminism as Andrea Dworkin
described it in 1974: The family must be destroyed, along with
normal sex roles — no more masculine men, no more feminine
women. Feminism is "a planetary movement to restructure
community forms and human consciousness," as Dworkin said.
Everything that exists must be destroyed in order for this feminist
revolution to succeed.

"Intercourse with men as we know them is increasingly impossible," Dworkin declared in 1974, and why? Because sexual intercourse for women "means acting out the female role," which Dworkin characterizes as one of "masochism, self-hatred, and passivity."

The reader will perhaps not be surprised to learn that Dworkin never had any children, and that her legal marriage to a homosexual man, John Stoltenberg, was an odd arrangement. "Stoltenberg had sexual relationships with other men throughout the course of his life with Dworkin," Ariel Levy explains. Stoltenberg never claimed to have had sex with Dworkin, who identified as a lesbian. "If Dworkin had not been his legal wife, she would not have been covered by his health insurance," Levy writes, in explaining why this odd couple married, "and the bills for the frequent surgeries and hospital stays that punctuated the end of her life would have left the couple in financial ruins."

To examine Andrea Dworkin's life and work is to understand what I mean when I say feminism is a journey to lesbianism. This is not an expression of stereotypical bigotry, but simply a way of saying that feminism — as a theory, as an ideology, as political philosophy — is implacably hostile to the normal woman's normal life of men, marriage and motherhood. One could rattle off a long list of pioneering feminist thinkers — Kate Millett, Shulamith Firestone, Dworkin, MacKinnon, on and on — without naming a woman who ever gave birth to a child. Hostility to marriage and motherhood is so essential to the feminist worldview that any woman who marries a man can be said to have abandoned the movement's basic principles. And certainly Andrea Dworkin was not the only feminist who saw that heterosexuality, involving as it does "ritualized behavior built on polar role definition," was incompatible with "the fundamental revolutionary commitment" of "ending male dominance." If lesbianism and feminism are not entirely synonymous, it is difficult to imagine how anyone who agrees with the claims Dworkin makes in *Intercourse* could think heterosexuality and feminism are compatible.

Male Sexuality as 'Goose-Stepping Hatred'

INTERCOURSE IS A BOOK DIFFICULT TO DESCRIBE, mainly because it is so distasteful to describe it. What it is, really, is a series of literary essays. Dworkin takes up the works of a number of male authors, classical and contemporary, and extracts from their writings passages that exhibit (or can be interpreted as exhibiting) what Dworkin considers the universal meaning of sexual intercourse. That is to say, Dworkin finds in these authors the expression of her idea that sex with men is inherently degrading to women, that sexual intercourse involves male dominance and a humiliation of women that is at least symbolic, if not deliberate. In Dworkin's reading, men desire intercourse with women only as a way to dehumanize women. Male sexuality in *Intercourse* is always predatory, if not violent, and Dworkin sees male sexuality as rooted in hateful contempt for women.

Most men and women recoil from Dworkin's hostility toward what, in their own experience, is a very enjoyable and loving act. And the careful reader of *Intercourse* cannot help but resent the literary trick she repeatedly plays: Here is this or that famous writer, talking about women and sex in an unpleasant way — of course, Dworkin implies, this is how *all* men view sex! It is certainly insulting to me, as a man, to find myself condemned on the basis of a novel I've never read, written by an author I have no reason to admire. Whatever my faults, how am I to blame for what Gustave Flaubert wrote in *Madame Bovary*?

This is Dworkin's *modus operandi*, a purposefully one-sided presentation. She has appointed herself the prosecuting attorney, as it were, against normal sexuality. Chapter One ("Repulsion") focuses on Leo Tolstoy; Chapter Two ("Skinless") is based on the Japanese novelist Kobo Abe; Chapter Three ("Stigma") takes on Tennessee Williams; Chapter Four ("Communion") involves James Baldwin; and in Chapter Five ("Possession") Dworkin focuses on Isaac Bashevis Singer. By the time you finish the first five chapters of Intercourse, you're past the 100-page mark, which is to say you've read more than 40 percent of this 250-page book, and practically every idea Dworkin has presented by this point is based on the writing of exactly five authors.

Dworkin is playing a trick, you see, and let's point out that two of the authors she chooses here — Williams and Baldwin — were both gay men; if their portrayals of women involve misogynistic contempt, such attitudes can hardly form the basis for a condemnation of heterosexuality. *Intercourse* begins with Tolstoy, whose marriage to Mrs. Tolstoy seems to have been rather unhappy.

Their letters and diaries are quoted to establish this, and then we get to Tolstoy's novel *The Kreutzer Sonata*, which involves a man who murders his wife. Dworkin writes:

A human life has been taken, horribly; a human being has done it. For this one moment, even the reader's interior rage at the author's full-blooded misogyny is stilled in sorrow. In contemporary books and films, the murder of a woman is an end in itself. In this sad story, the murder of the woman signifies the impossibility of physical love in a way that means loss, not sadistic celebration.

Tolstoy's repulsion for woman as such is not modern either. Now, this repulsion is literal and linear: directed especially against her genitals, also her breasts, also her mouth newly perceived as a sex organ. It is a goose-stepping hatred of cunt. The woman has no human dimension, no human meaning. The repulsion requires no explanation, no rationalization. She has no internal life, no human resonance; she needs no human interpretation. Her flesh is hated; she is it without more. The hatred is by rote, with no human individuation, no highfalutin philosophy or pedestrian emotional ambivalence. The repulsion is self-evidently justified by the physical nature of the thing itself; the repulsion inheres in what the thing is. For the male, the repulsion is sexually intense, genitally focused, sexually solipsistic, without any critical or moral self-consciousness. Photograph what she is, painted pink; the camera delivers her up as a dead thing; the picture is of a corpse, embalmed. The contemporary novelist does it with words: paints the thing, fucks it, kills it.

Tolstoy, in this story, locates his repulsion not in the woman's body, not in her inherent nature, but in sexual intercourse, the nature of the act: what it means; the inequality of the sexes intrinsic to it; its morbid consequences to the dignity and self-esteem of men.

The reader will notice here Dworkin's deliberate use of vulgarity — "cunt" and "fuck" — for shock value, attempting to convey to the reader the anti-female hatred she attributes to men. Notice also how, supposedly describing the "modern" view of the "contemporary novelist" (as contrasted with Tolstoy), Dworkin writes sentences about male "repulsion for women" that seem to be describing not merely a theme in literature, but rather stating the universal misogyny of men. Do men really feel this way toward women? Is male sexuality "hatred" toward women "by rote, with no human individuation," a feeling of repulsion that "is sexually intense, genitally focused"?

This is madness! And neither, for that matter, do I suppose that most men in Tolstoy's time dreaded women because they believed sexual intercourse had "morbid consequences to the dignity and self-esteem of men." Dworkin's claim that male sexuality involves "goose-stepping hatred of cunt" is as ridiculous as it is insulting, and her use of such a phrase reveals what *Intercourse* actually is, anti-male hate propaganda. The reader braces himself for Dworkin's encounter in Chapter Three with the ultimate man-beast:

> In *A Streetcar Named Desire*, Stanley Kowalski is a sexual animal, without self-consciousness, without introspection.
> …
> He is the prototypical male animal, without remorse. Each act of sex or act of animal exhibition of virility is nature, not art; in the realm of the inevitable, brute force, an ego that functions as part of the body's appetites.
> Having been beaten by him, his wife Stella waits for him, wanting him. She defends her willingness to accept the beating to her sister, Blanche Du Bois, who wants her to rebel: "But there are things that happen between a man and a woman in the dark — that sort of make everything else seem unimportant." The wife, raised to be refined, wants the animal passion of her husband, not anything else that she has had or could be. All her past of sensibility and taste means nothing to her against the way her husband uses her in the dark.

And? Your point is? We all make our choices in life. We all have our own tastes and preferences. Some women like bad boys. Some women don't much care for men who are civilized and thoughtful. And if their preference for savage men puts them at risk, whose fault is that? Being a skinny fellow myself, I might be accused of envy if I criticized women who go for the hulking Neanderthal type. So when her Neanderthal man pops her upside the head, what can I say, other than, "I told you so"? Anyway, back to Dworkin's take on *Streetcar*:

> Stanley's animal sexuality leaves him virtually untouched by the meaning of any experience because he has no

interior life, he is invulnerable to consequences, he has no memory past sensation. He is ordinary. Despite the radiant intensity of his sexuality, despite his wife's genteel refinement, despite the intensity of the sex between them, they are like everyone else. . . .
They have a habitual life of fucking and violence that blends into the common neighborhood life around them. . . . They conform perfectly to the patterns of the married people around them. The couple upstairs will have the same drama of battery and fucking in the course of the play; Stanley and Stella are a younger version, not different in quality or kind. Blanche is different. Blanche is marked, stigmatized, by her capacity to feel inside; by loneliness, vulnerability, despair; by her need for sex in conflict with her capacity for love; by her need for sex in conflict with what are the immediate needs of survival—passing as a real lady, not someone shopworn and used up, and marrying Mitch, Stanley's staid companion.

Wait, what is Blanche, actually? Isn't she basically a snob? Doesn't she represent a type of person whose pretensions and pride render them incapable of satisfaction in normal life? Isn't the reason *A Streetcar Named Desire* was such a huge success (and remains a classic) is because we all know types like Blanche? This is a work of literature, you see, and like all great literature, it involves characters who are familiar to us because they resemble actual people. Dworkin describes Blanche sympathetically:

Blanche's desire had always set her apart, because she always wanted a lover with a sensibility the opposite of Stanley's, not traditionally masculine, animalistic, aggressive; she always wanted someone in whom "some tenderer feelings have had some little beginning! " She was always Stanley's enemy, the enemy of the ordinary, however unrepressed the ordinary was. And it was this opposition to the ordinary — to ordinary masculinity — that marked her: that was her sexual appetite, her capacity to love, the anguish at the heart of her desire.

There is something tragic here, indeed. But somehow Dworkin has given it a political twist, so that while most people see Blanche as an unrealistic dreamer, maladjusted and hypocritical, Blanche's opposition to Stanley's "traditionally masculine, animalistic" sexuality makes her someone for whom Dworkin wishes us to have sympathy. Of course, this being a Southern Gothic tragedy, Stanley rapes Blanche, and her sister doesn't believe it, and Blanche has a nervous breakdown. Dworkin characterizes this turn of events:

> Stanley has Blanche taken away, institutionalized as mad, in the world of Tennessee Williams the worst consequence of sexual knowledge, the worst punishment, crueler than death.
>
> Because Stanley has no interior life of feeling, he has no remorse; the rape is just another fuck for him. It takes a human consciousness, including a capacity for suffering, to distinguish between a rape and a fuck. With no interior life of human meaning and human remorse, any fuck is simply expressive and animalistic, whatever its consequences or circumstances. Blanche pays the price for having a human sexuality and a human consciousness. She has been raped; she knows it. There is nothing in the text of the play, despite the way it is sometimes staged, to suggest that she wanted it all along. In fact, there is a pronounced and emotionally vivid history of her wanting its opposite — a sexuality of tenderness and sensitivity. She is taken away, locked up, because she knows what happened to her. . . . She is punished for knowing the meaning of what Stanley did to her because her capacity to know and to feel is his enemy. The rape itself was a revenge on her for wanting more than an animal fuck delivered by an animal masculinity: for feeling more, wanting more, knowing more. For her, sex was part of a human quest for human solace, human kindness . . . Stanley, ordinary, unrepressed, was the natural enemy of sex with any dimension of human longing or human meaning, any wanting that was not just for the raw, cold, hard fuck, a sensual using without any edge of loneliness or discontent. Blanche is marked, finally, by madness, jailed; not for her sexuality but for his, because his sexuality requires the annihilation of her aspirations to tenderness.

And? Your point is? These are real human beings. Or rather, they are representations of real human beings in a Southern Gothic play written in mid-20th-century America. Exactly how would Andrea Dworkin prefer the play to be scripted? We don't know. All we know is that, as scripted by Tennessee Williams, *A Streetcar Named Desire* represents to Dworkin . . . Well, something bad about men and sex, that's for sure. For her, *everything* represents something bad about men and sex.

'The Measure of Women's Oppression'

THE WORLD OF TENNESSEE WILLIAMS PLAYS is a world where dreams inevitably get crushed, and the dreamers along with them. The moral of the story is always, "Stop dreaming. Live in the real world." This is a pretty valuable message, really, but helpful life lessons from literature aren't what Andrea Dworkin wants. For her, the dream-crushing aspects of reality are a political cause, and the brute Stanley Kowalski is a symbol of the enemy, the typical male who annihilates women who want "more than an animal fuck."

Dworkin is the prosecuting attorney, and all men are defendants in this case, which resembles nothing so much as the Moscow "show trials" of the 1930s, where the paranoid Stalin purged his suspected rivals for power in the Soviet Union. Dworkin's paroxysms of hate reach their shuddering climax in Chapter Seven of *Intercourse*:

> The measure of women's oppression is that we do not take intercourse — entry, penetration, occupation — and ask or say what it means: to us as a dominated group or to us as a potentially free and self-determining people. Instead, intercourse is a loyalty test; and we are not supposed to tell the truth unless it compliments and upholds the dominant male ethos on sex. We know nothing, of course, about intercourse because we are women and women know nothing; or because what we know simply has no significance, entered into as we are. And men know everything — all of them — all the time — no matter how stupid or inexperienced or arrogant or ignorant they are. Anything men say on intercourse, any attitude they have, is valuable, knowledgeable, and deep, rooted in the cosmos and the forces of nature as it were: because they know; because fucking is knowing; because he knew her but she did not know him; because the God who does not exist framed not only sex but also knowledge that way.

Note how, in this passage, Dworkin shifts from "women's oppression" to ranting about men — "stupid or inexperienced or arrogant or ignorant" — and then ranting about God?

Her condemnation of men who claim to "know everything," who require that all discussion of sex must conform to "the dominant male ethos on sex," is directed at all men — "all of them — all the time." And what she clearly wants the reader to conclude is the opposite: MEN KNOW NOTHING.

It's a zero-sum game, you see.

Andrea Dworkin's feminism was not about equality with men. Equality would mean that at some point, there might be an occasion when a man could be right and Andrea Dworkin could be wrong.

Just as Blanche Du Bois was a type, so also was Andrea Dworkin a type — the fanatical self-righteous loudmouth type, who never once in her life admitted to any error, any fault or failure. Everybody in the world was always wrong, unless they agreed with her.

Here we have a woman whose anger at half the human race was her professional *raison d'etre*, for whom hatred of men was a litmus test of one's moral worth: If you did not hate men as much as she did, you were her inferior. And because nobody could ever hate men more than Andrea Dworkin did, this meant she was the most moral person on Earth. Conveniently, then, her worldview had the effect of making her better than everybody else, in her own mind.

Feminism is fundamentally inhumane. It is a totalitarian belief system, intolerant of dissent. It is a rationalization of hate, and therefore feminism can justify telling any lie, so long as men are hurt (and feminists are empowered) by the lie. By the time we reach Chapter Six of Intercourse ("Virginity"), Dworkin assumes the reader has already been convinced that sex is what she says it is — an expression of men's contempt for women — and the f-bombs come raining down as she discusses Flaubert's most famous creation, Emma of *Madame Bovary*:

> She has been fucked, she has wanted it, felt it, craved it, lost everything for it; and from it she has nothing, she is empty.
> . . . The intercourse itself, the submission it engenders in her, the habit of being that it becomes, the need she has for the pleasure it gives her, changes her without giving her any capacity to see, to know, or to love. Fucking leads to the loss of illusion, especially the illusion that love, sex, and sensation are the same as freedom, as heroism. Emma's

fantasies cannot stand up against the crushing reality of
male sexual dominance: the fucking, the boredom, the
abandonment.

Having never read Flaubert, I cannot say whether Dworkin's
interpretation of *Madame Bovary* is valid as literary criticism.
However, the reader recognizes that Dworkin is not merely
reviewing a French novel here. She is using this novel to condemn
men and to vent her rage at "the crushing reality of male sexual
dominance." Dworkin's book could be called *Fear and Loathing of
the Penis*. "The personal is the political," and for Dworkin, the
personal was horrific. As Ariel Levy writes in her foreword to
Intercourse, the "nightmarish pieces of [Dworkin's] reality were
picked over, deconstructed, and retold in everything she ever wrote":

If you have never experienced such things, it can be
difficult to relate to Dworkin. Sometimes, when you are
reading her work, it can seem almost impossible to
reconcile the world around you with the world on the page.

A nice touch, Ms. Levy — "*almost* impossible." A polite attempt to
rescue Dworkin's credibility. You see, however, that Dworkin
always insisted that the "world on the page" was a universal reality,
that all men do "such things" to all women. Dworkin did not say, "I
was brutalized by a Dutch anarchist, so avoid Dutch anarchists." No,
she turned her personal problems into a demand for a political
solution, calling for "a political action where revolu-tion is the goal,"
with destruction of the normal family as its first objective.

Like all of Dworkin's eulogists, Levy wants to rescue Dworkin,
to exempt her from responsibility for what she actually wrote, and
this is not to say that everything Dworkin wrote was wrong. In fact,
it was in Carolyn Graglia's excellent 1998 book *Domestic
Tranquility: A Brief Against Feminism* — which I highly
recommend — that I first encountered excerpts of Dworkin's
Intercourse. Mrs. Graglia confronted Dworkin's notorious work
head-on, speaking on behalf of normal women whose experience of
"male sexual dominance" is delightfully erotic. The man as
conquering hero, in a sexual context, is especially cherished by
normal women. To be passionately desired by the man she loves —
a man she respects, a man who has earned her trust — is by no
means humiliating to the normal woman. And as for "the submission
it engenders in her"? Well, yes.

Yes, yes, yes, says the normal woman in such a circumstance.

The man she loves is a man she respects and trusts. He is a civilized man — no brutal Dutch anarchist — but in the moment of his heroic conquest, the civilized man is transformed into a creature helpless to resist his own primal desire. We need not be surprised that the normal woman is pleased by his primal regression, knowing that it is she herself who has aroused the beast inside him. It is she who transforms him, she who peels away the mask of civilization her respectable man wears by habit.

He becomes the conquering hero and, in that moment, the civilized man is Stanley Kowalski. The woman experiences his "animal masculinity," just as Dworkin said, except that the normal woman loves it: *Yes, yes, yes!* Man and woman are equally helpless in that moment. They each become their natural selves, irrational and out of control, together experiencing each other in a way no one else can. His "sexual dominance" and "the submission it engenders in her" — *yes, yes, yes!*

Getting men and women to that place, that situation where "animal masculinity" can have its natural function under conditions of mutual respect, is the great challenge of civilization. Channeling human sexuality toward its rightful purpose, constraining the primal urge within a system of morality, so that man's desire becomes a beneficial force in society — this is the challenge which our customs, law and culture must meet, if we are not to descend into savagery, perversion, decadence and chaos. Feminism either refuses to recognize this challenge or, as in Dworkin's writing, feminism actively seeks to destroy civilization.

Dworkin in 1974 called for a revolution, condemning "conventional heterosexual behavior" and blaming the nuclear family for our "sexist, sexually repressed society." Dworkin declared "that 'man' and 'woman' are fictions . . . cultural constructs," and she proclaimed that rejection of the incest taboo was "essential" to achieving her feminist vision of "natural androgynous eroticism." None of Dworkin's posthumous defenders ever acknowledges or attempts to justify these revolutionary goals Dworkin laid out in her first feminist book, *Woman Hating*. There is a compulsive dishonesty about feminism that requires its adherents to avoid such topics. Why? Because if people knew the truth about feminism — if they knew who feminists really are and what feminists really want — the adherents of this perverse philosophy would be recognized as the hateful and twisted monsters they actually are, the enemies of all that is good and wholesome in human life.

Feminism is a synonym for hypocrisy and the antonym of intellectual integrity. If you did not understand the fundamental dishonesty of feminism, you might suppose Ariel Levy would have noticed the contradictions between what Andrea Dworkin wrote in 1974 and what Dworkin wrote in 1987. In 1974's *Woman Hating*, we find Dworkin demanding the abolition of the incest taboo, the recognition of children as "erotic beings," envisioning an androgynous future in which not only would male and female sex roles be eliminated, but also "distinctions between 'children' and 'adults' . . . would disappear."

What can Dworkin possibly mean by this, except what any reader can see she so obviously does mean? What Dworkin described in 1974 is what Matt Barber has rightly called "Sexual Anarchy," and here's the important point: She never took it back.

Dworkin never recanted, never apologized, never admitted that what she advocated in *Woman Hating* was a very dangerous idea.

The Esoteric Doctrine of Man-Hating

FEMINISM IS A FORMULA FOR IRRESPONSIBILITY. All that is necessary, in feminist rhetoric and belief, is to blame men for everything bad. As long as a feminist makes "male domination" her target — as long as she denounces the traditional family and Judeo-Christian morality, and makes men the scapegoats of her arguments — nothing else she says or does really matters.

By this standard (which is the only intellectual standard within feminism), Andrea Dworkin was the ultimate Good Feminist. As such, she could never be required to account for her dangerous ideas, never be expected to apologize for her errors. To be a feminist in good standing, therefore, requires a woman to ignore the basic errors of her fellow feminists, to cooperate in feminism's totalitarian project of silencing critics who call attention to that which feminism must ignore. This is why, after all, Larry Summers had to be hounded out of his job as president of Harvard University merely for suggesting that "innate differences" between men and women might explain the shortage of female scientists. If there are "innate differences" between men and women, you see, then feminism's vision of an androgynous future is wrong, and the attempt to bring about this sexless utopia — the planned outcome of feminism's war against human nature — is not only doomed to failure, but the policy "reforms" aimed at achieving this impossible goal are actually harmful to everyone, women included. If we recognize "innate differences" between men and women, we must also recognize that feminist policy will ultimately destroy all hope for human happiness.

For this reason, Ariel Levy's foreword to the 20th anniversary edition of Dworkin's *Intercourse* ignores the revolutionary aims of Dworkin's anti-male/anti-heterosexual ideology. The real purpose of Dworkin's arguments — the "political action where revolution is the goal," as the author had proclaimed in her first feminist book — must be ignored, and instead Levy would have us pay attention to the common accusations against Dworkin, *i.e.*, that she was a man-hater, and that *Intercourse* argues that "all sex is rape":

> Dworkin was accused of being a man-hater even by some members of her own movement. And she didn't write or make speeches with an eye toward mitigating this perception. In a speech she gave in Bryant Park at a "Take Back the Night" march in 1979, she called romance "rape embellished with meaningful looks."

Stipulate that Ariel Levy is not a bad writer. Her 2005 book *Female Chauvinist Pigs: Women and the Rise of Raunch Culture* has been recommended to me by several (anti-feminist) readers as a critique of "pro-sex feminism" and the "Girls Gone Wild" *ethos* we might describe as Empowerment Through Promiscuity. And in addressing the common accusations against Dworkin, Levy more or less admits Dworkin's accusers are right: Her hostility to normal male sexuality was such that there was, in Dworkin's mind, a continuum of coercion in every heterosexual experience for women. Our ordinary understanding of "consent" — the idea that women genuinely desire sex with men, and are capable of rationally acting on their desires — is false, according to Dworkin's feminist theory. If the roles of men and women are "cultural constructs," as Dworkin declared (and as all feminists believe), then the attitudes, beliefs and behaviors associated with those roles are also "constructed" by a society and culture which are male-dominated. Therefore, feminism teaches, the only reason women consent to sex is because they have been trained and indoctrinated to consent, and thus romance (*i.e.*, women's performance of their prescribed role) is merely "rape embellished with meaningful looks."

Normal women instinctively recoil from feminism when they are told what it really means, and what feminists really believe. Feminism is inherently radical, based on a revolutionary interpretation of human behavior, and must either be accepted or rejected as such. Feminists know this, and they understand that their success depends on a hypocritical duality between their movement's *esoteric* doctrine (feminism's radical theory) and its *exoteric* discourse (the language feminists speak to the general public).

This necessary gap between the esoteric and exoteric meanings of feminism explains why the typical college sophomore who signs up for a fall-semester Introduction to Women's Studies class — a humanities elective, in which she expects to get an easy "A" — is seldom aware of what she's getting herself into. Maybe she thinks of herself as a "feminist" in a very ordinary and superficial sense of that word (*"Vote Democrat, because vagina!"*), but the 19-year-old who shows up for the first day of Introduction to Women's Studies in August or September doesn't realize what actual feminism will require her to believe. No one tells her that the editors of the assigned textbook are radical lesbians. Our typical sophomore has not critically researched feminism; when she glances through the bibliographies and indexes of the books she is assigned, the college girl doesn't recognize the names of authors the way she should: "*Michel Foucault*, the gay man who died of AIDS; *Bettina Aptheker*, apologist for genocidal Marxist dictators; *Gayle Rubin*, the advocate of lesbian sadomasochism; *Simone de Beauvoir*, the French pervert who seduced schoolgirls and defended pedophilia . . ."

She doesn't know who these people actually are or were, and does not confront their core beliefs on the first day of class. Instead, her Women's Studies professor leads the naive sophomore through a carefully planned sequence of readings and lectures. She is presented with Premise A (male oppression under patriarchy) and then Premise B (gender is a social construct) of the feminist syllogism, so that by the time in late October or early November when the argument arrives at its obvious conclusion — "If A, then B, ergo C, you must be a lesbian" — she may reject feminism's logical requirement, but she is unable to justify her rejection rationally. Her lesbian professor has spent weeks setting her up for this, undermining any justification of heterosexuality as a natural, normal and desirable way of life. Under the tutelage of a 40-year-old Ph.D., the 19-year-old sophomore is compelled to believe that what she is taught in

Women's Studies is Truth with a capital "T" and Science with a capital "S." Nothing in the sophomore's knowledge or experience has prepared her to cope with her professor's Scientific Truth, and this unexpected confrontation leaves the young feminist with the sense that a normal woman's normal life of men, marriage and motherhood is unworthy, oppressive, scientifically invalid. She may not become a lesbian (her heterosexuality cannot be entirely "deconstructed" in a single semester), but she can never thereafter be wholly satisfied with a normal life. Feminism teaches women that to be normal is to be inferior.

All feminists must collaborate to uphold the partition that conceals feminism's esoteric doctrine from critical public scrutiny. Forthright radicals like Andrea Dworkin are therefore viewed as dangerous to the feminist project. Sitting here at my desk surrounded by dozens of feminist books — including such titles as *Theorizing Sexuality*, *Women and Gender*, and *The Social Construction of Lesbianism* — I understand what so-called "mainstream feminists" fear about Dworkin, who so often said in bold sentences what all true feminists must privately believe.

We may smile at Ariel Levy's sentence: "Dworkin was accused of being a man-hater even by some members of her own movement."

Irony much? Whence the feminist movement's fear of the "man-hater" label? Because feminism can never openly admit the truth — the movement's esoteric doctrine, which is not only anti-male but also anti-heterosexual — to the general public. If the truth of the feminist cult's metaphysical theories were admitted and recognized, exposed to the uninitiated who have not subscribed to the cultic *gnosis*, people would begin to ask why these dangerous hateful doctrines are being promulgated at taxpayer expense in public university classrooms.

If the truth about feminism were widely known, we might see more instances of what happened this year in South Carolina, where the legislature defunded a state university "Women's Center" that had staged an event called "How to Be a Lesbian in 10 Days or Less." (The director of that program is a mentally ill lesbian Ph.D. who married one of her female students.) All that is necessary to defeat feminism is to tell the truth about feminism. Quote what feminists write when they are writing for an intended readership of their fellow feminists.

Ariel Levy, in her 2007 foreword to the 20th anniversary edition of Dworkin's *Intercourse*, could only briefly allude to Dworkin's first book, 1974's *Woman Hating*. It would not be helpful to the feminist movement to remind readers what absurdities Dworkin wrote about witches and fairies, about "erotic" children and abolishing the incest taboo. No, this would not do, because it seems some people actually believed that stuff. On the final pages of *Intercourse* (pp. 246-247), Dworkin quotes an incest survivor — horrifying words, a quote I will omit — before making her concluding accusation against men:

> The men as a body politic have power over women and decide how women will suffer: which sadistic acts against the bodies of women will be construed to be normal. In the United States, incest is increasingly the sadism of choice, the intercourse itself wounding the female child and socializing her to her female status — early; perhaps a sexual response to the political rebellion of adult women; a tyranny to destroy the potential for rebellion. . . . Perhaps incestuous rape is becoming a central paradigm for intercourse in our time. Women are supposed to be small and childlike, in looks, in rights; child prostitution keeps increasing in mass and in legitimacy, the children sexually used by a long chain of men — fathers, uncles, grandfathers, brothers, pimps, pornographers, and the good citizens who are the consumers; and men, who are, after all, just family, are supposed to slice us up the middle, leaving us in parts on the bed.

Those are the final words of Andrea Dworkin's most famous book, published in 1987, barely a dozen years after Dworkin's first book had extended *carte blanche* to child molesters, evidently because in 1974 she viewed pedophiles as feminism's natural allies in "a political action where revolution is the goal," where the destruction of the normal family was an objective requiring the abolition of the incest taboo.

By 1987, the feminist revolution had already done much "to restructure community forms and human consciousness," as promiscuity, divorce, abortion and homosexuality proliferated. But feminists had to exculpate themselves from responsibility for the accompanying plague of other evils — rape and incest, pornography and prostitution — that anyone with common sense could have predicted would result from the revolution. Therefore, by the late 1980s, Dworkin needed an elaborate argument to blame all these evils on feminism's scapegoat, the male-dominated society.

Ariel Levy could not remind readers that what Andrea Dworkin denounced in 1987 as an atrocity of male "tyranny" was, in fact, a predictable consequence of an ideology Dworkin avowed in 1974.

Any intelligent reader can see what Dworkin was doing in *Intercourse*, deliberately and falsely making all males ("men as a body politic") complicit in the worst crimes imaginable. Any intelligent reader, arriving at the conclusion of Dworkin's 1987 book, realizes that her cruel and dishonest conclusion exposes the entire book as a monstrous lie. Only the coldest hatred could have motivated Dworkin to write that final paragraph. Only a women utterly without conscience could have blamed "men as a body politic" for these heinous crimes in 1987, knowing how she herself had implicitly endorsed incest and pedophilia in 1974.

Our laws impose severe punishments on rapists, especially on rapists who victimize children. It is certainly no accident that Dworkin wished to cast the shadow of suspicion on all men as complicit in such crimes, for this is what hate propaganda does. Feminism is a doctrine of hatred that scapegoats and demonizes half the human race (males), while also stigmatizing normal women (heterosexual females, especially in their roles as wives and mothers) as untrustworthy collaborators with male "tyranny." Dworkin was one of the most successful propagandists of feminism's ideology of hate, because she was skillful at the dishonest methods of rhetoric required for success in that endeavor. Only a careful and skeptical reader would notice the significance of Dworkin's concluding paragraph in *Intercourse* or remark how she composes a list that lumps together "fathers, uncles, grandfathers, brothers . . . and the good citizens" with pimps and pornographers. Her implied meaning is obvious enough: All men are guilty of rape and incest, all men are responsible for pornography and prostitution, despite the fact that Dworkin herself and the feminist movement as a whole have allied themselves against every institution of society that seeks to enforce the moral code (as religion, as culture, as law and custom) which might restrain the dangerous forces of anarchistic sexual hedonism.

"They are without excuse," as the Bible says. If "incestuous rape is becoming a central paradigm" and "child prostitution keeps increasing in mass and in legitimacy," as Andrea Dworkin wrote in concluding her 1987 book, how could she exempt herself from blame, considering what she wrote on these topics in her 1974 book? Yet Dworkin in 1987 writes as if the Dworkin of 1974 never existed and, in 2007, Ariel Levy continued that phony feminist charade of pretended ignorance.

All good and decent people must despise such hateful hypocrisy, just as all honest people must condemn it, but Andrea Dworkin was not good or decent or honest. Andrea Dworkin was a feminist.

The Crazy Feminism
of Joyce Trebilcot

AMERICA LOST A VALUABLE SOURCE of feminist craziness when Professor Joyce Trebilcot died in 2009 at age 74. For more than three decades, Trebilcot supplied the feminist movement with its necessary raw material — insanity — and in its obituary of this distinguished academic, Washington University St. Louis described her contributions:

> Trebilcot, who joined the University in 1970 as assistant
> professor of philosophy, helped found the women's studies major
> in 1972 and the program in 1975. She served as coordinator of
> the program from 1980-1992. . . .
> "Working with a group of committed students and faculty, Joyce
> Trebilcot played an integral role in developing women's studies
> at Washington University from a special major into an
> interdisciplinary program in the 1970s," said Mary Ann
> Dzuback, Ph.D., associate professor and director of the Women,
> Gender and Sexuality Studies Program. . . .
> A founding member of the Society for Women in Philosophy and
> of the editorial board of Hypatia: A Journal of Feminist
> Philosophy, Trebilcot grew up in Oakland, Calif., and earned a
> bachelor's degree from the University of California, Berkeley,
> and a doctorate from the University of California, Santa Barbara.

Professor Trebilcot left behind a lesbian widow, her partner Jan Crites, as well as a formidable body of insane feminist writings. Perhaps most widely cited was her influential 1974 treatise "Sex Roles: The Argument From Nature," a landmark work of lunatic feminism.

Addressing herself to the question of whether male/female sex roles are justified by "natural psychological differences between the sexes," Professor Trebilcot in effect answered, "So what?"

> In this paper I argue that whether there are natural psychological
> differences between females and males has little bearing on the
> issue of whether society should reserve certain roles for females
> and others for males. . . .
> The question is, after all, not what women and men naturally are,
> but what kind of society is morally justifiable. In order to answer
> this question, we must appeal to the notions of justice, equality,
> and liberty. It is these moral concepts, not the empirical issue of
> sex differences, which should have pride of place in the
> philosophical discussion of sex roles.

OK, so "what kind of society is morally justifiable"?

If you ask a lesbian feminist that question, you might not be surprised that her answer is "lesbian feminist society," and Professor Trebilcot seems to have dedicated much of her career to that proposition. Her 1994 book *Dyke Ideas: Process, Politics, Daily Life* is a collection of essays devoted to Professor Trebilcot's gynocentric philosophy. One of her essays in that volume, "Dyke Methods, or Principles for the Discovery/Creation for the Withstanding," was first published in the feminist journal *Hypatia* in 1988. It begins with Professor Trebilcot's statement that she is "alarmed by the domination inherent in the patriarchal idea of truth." She states her purpose thus:

> The methods I discuss in this essay are, most narrowly
> conceived, methods for using language. They are, therefore,
> methods for a great deal else as well — experiencing, thinking,
> acting. But my focus is on language, on verbal language, on
> English; my focus is on how, as a dyke — a conscious,
> committed, political lesbian — I can use words in thinking,
> speaking, and writing to contribute to the discovery/creation of
> consciously lesbian realities.

To a student of psychology, this looks suspiciously like "magic thinking" and "word salad," typical symptoms of schizophrenia. Yet keep in mind that this was written by a tenured professor who, at the time, was serving as coordinator of her university Women's Studies program.

Among the inmates of our nation's mental hospitals are perhaps thousands of women who, if handed a Ph.D. in philosophy, could get tenure-track positions under the standards that prevailed in the Women's Studies programs of the 1970s, when it seemed that any crazy lesbian like Professor Trebilcot (or Mary Daly or Sally Miller Gearhart) could become an academic superstar. This explains why feminism, unlike some other fads of its era, has proven so remarkably persistent. It's hard to make a career of tie-dyed T-shirts and bell-bottom pants, but being a professional crazy lesbian? The National Women's Studies Association is dedicated to making such careers possible. The teenage lesbian with no skills (other than an aptitude for "critical theory" jargon) and no interest in getting an actual *job* can become a Women's Studies major at her college and at least hope that her avid emulation of feminism's founding foremothers will qualify her to teach this lunatic nonsense to other disturbed young women. Alternatively, she can apply for a job as a hotel desk clerk, or work for a nonprofit like the Feminist Majority Foundation. If all else fails, she can become a radical feminist blogger and proclaim to the world: *"PIV is always rape, OK?"*

We can perceive a Continuum of Feminist Insanity, as we might call it, between (a) pioneering lunatics like Joyce Trebilcot and (b) the crazy feminists who turned a (non-existent) "rape epidemic" on college campuses into California's "affirmative consent" law, enacted in September 2014. What has happened is that unrealistic beliefs about men, women and sex have obtained intellectual prestige. These beliefs have gained institutional authority from the hegemonic influence of feminism within academia and, inevitably, once the lunatics took over the asylum, they acquired political power sufficient to legislate crazy laws.

Quod erat demonstrandum.

How has this happened? You see that in the 1970s, when the first Women's Studies programs were created, this enabled obscure academic mediocrities — previously undistinguished women who happened to have obtained advanced degrees in the humanities and social sciences — suddenly to become superstars within the universe of Official Feminism. All that was necessary, to a feminist with a Ph.D. and a faculty sinecure, was to write articles and books that espoused feminist ideals and made arguments politically useful to feminism's goals. No argument was too ludicrous for publication, if it served a feminist purpose. Joyce Trebilcot's 1974 argument about sex roles, for example, wasn't so much an argument (in the sense of formal logic) as it was a crude bait-and-switch: Begin by discussing evidence regarding general psychological differences between men and women and then — *abracadabra!* — declare that the differences don't matter, because "notions of justice, equality, and liberty" are more important than facts.

As a formula for insanity, feminism rivals LSD in its potency.

Permit me to digress. It has always been my belief, based on extensive youthful experience with crazy dopeheads, that Mary Daly must have had at least a few LSD trips. Anyone who has hung around acid freaks could pick up a copy of Professor Daly's most famous book, *Gyn/Ecology: The Metaethics of Radical Feminism*, and recognize the telltale signs she was tripping when she wrote it or, at least, Daly had done enough serious hallucinogens to acquire that permanent propensity for Cosmic Metaphysical Gibberish that longtime freaks typically display.

This is a digression, I say, but not entirely irrelevant to understanding the fundamental unrealism of feminist thought. Every author who writes about the origins of so-called "Second Wave" feminism in the late 1960s routinely observes the historical context of the movement's roots in the radical New Left, including the civil rights and anti-war movements. What the historians generally fail to mention, however, is that the emergence of feminism also occurred at time when heavy experimentation with hallucinogens was commonplace among young radicals. You take a bright young bohemian — somebody with a 140 IQ, an antipathy to conventional authority and a penchant for theoretical abstraction — and supply that alienated young student with marijuana, LSD, psilocybin and other tools for "expanding their consciousness," and I guarantee the result will include craziness.

You can't really understand the etiology of feminism, I contend, if you ignore the Drug Factor. Perhaps not every radical woman of that era was a user of hallucinogens, but there were obviously enough Cosmic Space Travelers among them to form a critical mass of craziness.

'Ecstatic Communion' in Berkeley

"WHEN THE GOING GETS WEIRD, the weird turn pro," Hunter S. Thompson famously observed, and the revolutionary vanguard of the Women's Liberation movement clearly included some professional weirdos. And this brings us back to the subject of Professor Joyce Trebilcot's distinctive brand of feminist craziness. The 1988 feminist book *For Lesbians Only: A Separatist Anthology* includes an essay by Professor Trebilcot entitled "Craziness as a Source of Separatism." This provides helpful bits of autobiographical information:

> I begin with a brief description of the events I label "being crazy." I am remembering my life of the late 1950s and early 1960s, when I was in my late twenties. . . .
> There were two stages. First, intrusion. Men — male voices — would overhear my thoughts and want to get in. The second stage was control. The invaders not only wanted to get in, they wanted to take me over once they were in . . . This then is the core of the craziness — invasion and control, and the threat of invasion and control.
> I was drawn to participate, to allow the connection to happen, but at the same time I would repeatedly block. I was drawn because of the lightness and power of participation, and because of my values — acquired primarily in Berkeley during the "Beatnik" time as a street person and student of dance and philosophy — which made participating in "ecstatic communion," whether through drugs or religion or art or sex or some other means, the highest and consuming priority. Consciously, I accepted this "experience ethic" . . . but nevertheless . . . I would regularly block when it seemed that intense, shared experience was in the offing.
> As a result, I was in almost continuous emotional turmoil. I cried a lot, and punished myself, and traveled, moving repeatedly to new places in order to try again with new groups of people.

Hmmm. The future feminist professor was, in "the late 1950s and early 1960s," located "in Berkeley during the 'Beatnik' time." It was in this context that young Joyce Trebilcot acquired her "values" while "participating in 'ecstatic communion' . . . through drugs," etc.

What does the phrase "ecstatic communion" signify? Google searches for that phrase turn up a lot of New Age mystical stuff, some of it related to tantric Buddhism. In a book by David Deming, we find this reference to 11th-century Islamic philosopher Al-Ghazali:

> Al-Ghazali considered the possibility that this third way of knowing, the one that might be superior to ratiocination, was the mystic or ecstatic communion experienced by the Sufis. It was "a state in which, absorbed into themselves and in the suspension of sense-perceptions, they have visions beyond the reach of intellect."
>
> Known variously as illumination, ecstatic communion, or intuitive knowledge, mystic communion is an experience "of a supreme, all-pervading, and indwelling power, in whom all things are one." Mystic communion is the basis of revelation, prophecy, and religion. It is one of the most powerful forces in human history, and also one of the least understood.

Significantly, Al-Ghazali's thoughts about "ecstatic communion" occur in a treatise that Deming describes as "a refutation of Neoplatonic Aristotelianism." That is to say, this mystical idea of "intuitive knowledge" arises from an intellectual rejection of the Greek philosophical foundations of Western scientific thought. And according to Joyce Trebilcot, this idea of "ecstatic communion" was popular among the bohemian Beatniks of Berkeley in the late 1950s and early '60s, when she was forming her values.

Did I mention Professor Trebilcot is a lesbian? And did I mention that her essay "Craziness as a Source of Separatism" is about rape?

What she seems to have been describing, in terms of male "intrusion and control," was her dissatisfaction with the experience of heterosexuality as a 20-something woman amid the hedonistic Beatnik bohemians of Berkeley. She was "hearing the voices of men trying to rape me," she explains, and when she says she "would regularly block," it seems this phrase refers to her inability to achieve psychosexual satisfaction in her experiences with men at that time:

> I now understand all these refusals as resistances to rape, that is, to invasion and control by others.
>
> My interpretation of these experiences has shifted over the years. At the most painful time, it seemed to me that what was going on was that I wanted to do what they wanted me to, I wanted to participate in what was going on, but I simply could not, I was unable, I did not know how. I now understand this nonparticipation not as inability, but as refusal: it is not that I could not take part, but that I would not. And the reason I would not is that I wanted to protect myself from the assault, from the intrusion, from the loss of my own will. . . . I resisted in order to

continue as an individual — in order not be submerged, subjected, merged.

The patriarchal term "crazy" applies to all this, first, because I was certainly behaving in ways Western patriarchy takes to be typical of craziness — raving and crying. And when I talked about what was happening to me, my talk was "crazy talk." . . . One who just merges and submerges is not crazy, and one who just refuses isn't either. . . .

This resistance to control . . . is a preparation for lesbian separatism.

The most literal reading of this text would be that Trebilcot's "nonparticipation" means she rejected all male advances, but I suspect she also may be describing as "resistances" her inability to *enjoy* sex with men even when she consented to it amid that Beatnik culture where "ecstatic communion" was the goal, and her experiences weren't exactly ecstatic. Doing drugs and getting humped by a smelly existentialist art student, maybe? Not the sort of thing to inspire ecstasy, and you see Trebilcot talking about how her "interpretation of these experiences has shifted over the years" — feminist subjectivity now "empowering" her to view her Beatnik experiences as rape two decades later. Behavior that was judged crazy ("raving and crying") circa 1962, Trebilcot wished readers to believe more than 20 years later, was actually symptomatic of her "resistance to control," an early manifestation of the lesbianism she did not adopt as her identity until after the feminist revolution made lesbianism socially acceptable.

In her 20s, she was merely unhappy and viewed by others as crazy; by the time she reached her 40s, however, feminism had taught her (a) that her unhappiness was caused by "Western patriarchy," (b) that she was a lesbian, and (c) that the men who seduced her (or tried to seduce her) in her Beatnik youth were actually rapists.

As soon as I say this, I know someone will Google up an image of an elderly and unattractive Joyce Trebilcot, but I'm prepared to stipulate that the young Trebilcot was reasonably attractive. She was, however, a sort of bookish young lady, a distinct type of female one encounters who lacks the *animal vigor* necessary to overcome civilized inhibitions, who can't stop *thinking* and just *do it* with the passionate sense of abandonment required to achieve psychosexual satisfaction. That primitive "me Tarzan, you Jane" sexuality first requires Jane to attract the jungle man, and then to shed her self-consciousness in experiencing his savage masculinity in its most basic expression.

By the time Trebilcot was in her 40s, and writing about "the philosophical discussion of sex roles," she had clearly arrived at her logical destination: Feminism is a journey to lesbianism. What was "crazy talk" in 1962 was profound scholarly wisdom by 1974.

The fact that few people outside academia recognize the name Joyce Trebilcot should not lead us to believe that she was not influential, nor should we suppose that a professor who retired in 1995 has no relevance for the meaning of feminism today. What Professor Trebilcot discussed as "sex roles" in 1974, after all, is the same basic idea now known as Gender Theory, and such pioneers of academic feminism promoted concepts that have far-reaching impact in the 21st century. Consider, just as one example, University of Wisconsin Professor Claudia Card. From her Wikipedia page:

> She earned her BA from the University of Wisconsin–Madison (1962) and her MA (1964) and Ph.D. (1969) from Harvard University, where she wrote her dissertation under the direction of John Rawls. Joining the faculty in the philosophy department at Wisconsin straight from her Harvard studies, Card has been a significant voice there, and in the profession, ever since.
>
> Although securely rooted in and dedicated to Wisconsin, Card has held visiting professorships at The Goethe Institute (Frankfurt, Germany), Dartmouth College (Hanover NH), and the University of Pittsburgh. Card has written 4 treatises, edited or co-edited 6 books, published nearly 150 articles and reviews. She has delivered nearly 250 papers at conferences, colleges, and universities and has been featured in 29 radio broadcasts. In 2013, Card was invited to deliver the prestigious Paul Carus Lectures, a series of 3 lectures delivered to the American Philosophical Association; these will be delivered at the Central Division in 2016. She delivered the John Dewey Lecture to the Central APA in 2008. In April 2011 Card became the President of the APA's Central Division.

Professor Card is a very prestigious philosopher, you see, and in 1995, her book *Lesbian Choices* was published by Columbia University Press. This is from her book's bibliography, page 298:

> Trebilcot, Joyce. "Conceiving Women: Notes on the Logic of Feminism." *Sinister Wisdom* 11 (Fall 1979):43-50.
> Trebilcot, Joyce. "Notes on the Meaning of Life." *Lesbian Ethics* 1, no. 1 (Fall 1984):90-91.
> Trebilcot, Joyce. "Taking Responsibility for Sexuality." In *Philosophy and Sex*, 2d ed., ed. Robert Backer and Frederick Elliston. Buffalo, N.Y.: Prometheus, 1984.
> Trebilcot, Joyce. "Hortense and Gladys on Dreams." *Lesbian Ethics* 1, no. 2 (Spring 1985):85-87.

Trebilcot, Joyce. "Partial Response to Those Who Worry That Separatism May Be a Political Cop-Out: Expanded Definition of Activism." *off our backs* (May 1986). Reprinted in *Gossip* 3 (n.d.):82-84.

Trebilcot, Joyce. "Dyke Economics: Hortense and Gladys on Money." *Lesbian Ethics* 3, no. 1 (Spring 1988):1-13

Trebilcot, Joyce. "Dyke Methods." *Hypatia* 5, no. 1 (Spring 1990):1-13.

Trebilcot, Joyce. "More Dyke Methods." *Hypatia* 5, no. 3 (Fall 1990):147-52.

Trebilcot, Joyce. "Stalking Guilt." *Lesbian Ethics* 5, no. 1 (Summer 1993):72-75.

In case you lost count, *nine* separate works by Joyce Trebilcot were cited in this 300-page book by the influential Professor Card, a book published by a prestigious academic press. Thus were these various works that Professor Trebilcot published between 1979 and 1993 incorporated into the framework of Professor Card which in turn, we may be sure, has been cited by numerous other feminist scholars since.

By this incremental process — articles by professors little known outside the world of academic feminism, published in obscure journals and anthologies seldom read by anyone outside the scholarly echo chamber of Women's Studies — has feminism erected its intellectual Tower of Babel. And feminism's power on campus is such that no administrator, professor or student dares challenge it.

Acquiring intellectual respectability through the accretion of essays, articles, conference papers and books, academic feminism acquires its scholarly pedigree. Women's Studies, a field that did not exist before the 1970s, has created for itself a vast stockpile of academic resources, recognized works which appear in the notes and bibliographies of new works produced in the publish-or-perish process by which graduate students gain advanced degrees, and by which junior faculty prove themselves worthy of career advancement.

Crazy-Hating the Demonized Male Scapegoat

IT HAS BEEN CALCULATED THAT about 90,000 students enroll annually in Women's Studies classes at American colleges and universities, and there are thousands of instructors and professors paid to teach these courses. The Feminist-Industrial Complex, as I have called it, thus comprises a vast enterprise that exercises hegemonic power in academia, arrogating to itself the authority to speak about men, women, sex, marriage and family, so that any campus discourse on these topics is subject to being vetoed or silenced if it does not comport with feminist theory. The feminist lunatics are running the asylum of higher education, and no one should be surprised by the episodic outbreaks of craziness that result.

In June 2014, George Will, a Pulitzer-winning columnist for the *Washington Post*, criticized the anti-male hysteria of the phony "rape epidemic" on college campuses and, when he arrived to speak at Miami University of Ohio in October 2014, he was greeted by an angry mob of crazy women, claiming that this eminent journalist is objectively pro-rape. Yet I would wager $20 that of those campus protesters, fewer than half had actually read the column that made Will a demonized scapegoat, an Official Symbol of Misogyny. Nor would any of them, if you handed them a copy of his column, be able to explain cogently what was wrong with it, other than Will's claim that "when [colleges and universities] make victimhood a coveted status that confers privileges, victims proliferate." This claim appears in the second sentence of Will's column and several hundred words later — having mustered evidence to support his bold claim — Will writes in his penultimate paragraph:

> Academia is learning that its attempts to create victim-free
> campuses — by making everyone hypersensitive, even
> delusional, about victimizations — brings increasing supervision
> by the regulatory state that progressivism celebrates.

What he is talking about, in his reference to "the regulatory state," are interventions by the federal Department of Education, attempting to dictate to college administrators how they should handle claims of sexual misconduct by students. Officials justified this unprecedented intervention, as Will noted, by phony statistics that created the artificial appearance of a "rape epidemic" on campus when, in fact, data from other federal sources (the Department of Justice and the FBI) clearly show a *decline* in sexual assault during the past two decades. So the campus proliferation of victimhood — that is, college females who say they have been victimized — is a product resulting from the spread of an ideology (feminism) that incentivizes such claims "by making everyone hypersensitive." The difference between an unhappy drunken hook-up and an accusation of rape? In many cases, it appears to be a matter of subjective interpretation, especially if universities "make victimhood a coveted status that confers privileges." Notice that this is a general accusation Will makes against universities; he does not claim to know whether any particular woman was raped or not. He is claiming that our institutions of higher learning make victimhood a "status . . . that confers privilege." You can believe that or not, but you cannot fairly argue that George Will is *pro-rape* for writing it.

In the same way Joyce Trebilcot re-interpreted with feminist hindsight her experiences among the Beatniks in Berkeley, so has rape been re-interpreted by Trebilcot's young academic heiresses. And it is certainly no coincidence that many of the campus feminists — both faculty and students — who are shouting most loudly about "rape culture" are lesbians. Since the 1970s, radical feminists have insisted that women's sexuality is a matter of choice, but that lesbianism is a conscious, self-affirming, empowering (and therefore *legitimate*) choice, whereas female heterosexuality is "socially constructed" so that the heterosexual woman is a victim of patriarchal culture, misled into believing that her sexual preference for men is natural.

In her 1984 essay "Taking Responsibility for Sexuality," Joyce Trebilcot criticizes the belief that "one's sexuality . . . is inherited, or acquired in childhood . . . something that happens to you." Such a view of sexuality "tends to keep you docile: you are passive, submissive, with respect to it," Trebilcot explains, thus denying women the ability "to participate in the creating of our own sexual identities":

> As those familiar with feminist theory know, feminists advocate
> lesbianism on a variety of grounds. Some emphasize, for
> instance, that [on the basis of Freud's Oedipal theory of mother-
> love] lesbianism is "natural" for women, as heterosexuality is for
> men. Another approach is based on the claim that in patriarchy,
> equality in a heterosexual relationship is impossible. . . . A third
> argument holds that women committed to feminism should give
> all their energies to women. . . .
> I am particularly concerned here with women's taking
> responsibility for our sexual identities as lesbian or
> heterosexuality. . . .
> A paradigm case of taking responsibility for one's sexuality is
> coming out as a lesbian. It is characteristic . . . that a woman does
> not know whether to say that she has discovered that she is a
> lesbian, or that she has decided to be a lesbian. . . . In coming out,
> one connects an already-existing reality — sensations, feelings,
> identification with women — with a new understanding or
> concept of who one is. . . .
> To discover that one has been a lesbian all along is to interpret
> past experiences in a new way. . . . But coming out involves also
> deciding to be a lesbian, which is to say deciding not to
> participate in the institution of heterosexuality and to . . . love
> women. . . .
> Patriarchy, although it takes different forms in different cultures,
> always depends on the ability of men to control women through
> heterosexuality. . . . Were large numbers of women to take
> responsibility for our own sexuality and in doing so reject
> heterosexuality, the very concepts of woman and man would be
> shattered.

Professor Trebilcot was crazy, not stupid. The reader gets the message —
men *bad*, lesbians *good* — because lesbianism is described in positive
terms, as an exciting new thing "discovered," self-affirming and
responsible. By contrast, female heterosexuality is presented as routine
participation in a lifeless "institution" through which men control women.
Trebilcot's presentation is as tendentious as a sales pitch (*Discover Your
Exciting New Lesbian Self!*), inciting women to reject male control, "take
responsibility" and "love women."

Post-Oedipal Parents: Lesbian Motherhood

Anyone who is "familiar with feminist theory," as Professor Trebilcot said,
not only knows that feminists advocate lesbianism, but also that they have
expended many thousands of words either attacking Freudian theories or
else trying to turn the Oedipal conflict into an argument to justify
lesbianism as women's authentic and "natural" sexuality as Professor
Trebilcot said.

Freudianism has always struck me as ludicrous, but in wading through
dozens of volumes of feminist theory over the past few months, I have seen
author after author devote herself either to debunking Freud or adapting his
theories to feminist purposes. You see this most obviously when it comes
to the subject of lesbian motherhood.

There are obvious problems in trying to "deconstruct" parenting and
childhood to fit feminist theory. Now witness a feminist author, University
of California-Davis Professor Maureen Sullivan, employ Freudian
concepts in her 2004 book *The Family of Woman: Lesbian Mothers, Their
Children, and the Undoing of Gender*:

> Do lesbian mothers sexually "other" their sons? . . . In traditional
> psychoanalytic formulations the sexual otherness of boys/men
> derives not only from their having different sexual organs but
> from the desirability of the phallus as representing power,
> privilege, and pleasure. . . .
> Even though lesbian mothers and their children live in a
> heteronormative world where the phallus represents power,
> privilege, and often pleasure, these cultural meanings do not
> necessarily hold sway in the lesbian mother household. Bay Area
> mother Jill Collins had this to say about her three-year-old son's
> growing awareness of genitality:

> > He takes showers with me on a regular basis because I find
> > that's the most convenient way to bathe him. He's been
> > talking about his penis. And [his friend] James's penis. And
> > my penis. And I keep telling him I don't have one, you
> > know, and he likes to look, and now he's saying, "Jillie
> > doesn't have a penis. Mommy doesn't have a penis. Auntie

Kate doesn't have a penis. James has a penis. John has a penis. Danny has a penis." He's got it! Except for he really doesn't know what that means. He knows where his is, but he can't know where mine isn't. It's like he doesn't see that it's not there you know.

If it is safe to assume that lesbian parents have no need to develop libidinal investments in boy children, then the argument that heterosexual mothers "push" preoedipal sons into libidinally tinged oedipal dynamics because sons are "like father/male partner" will not hold for them. Moreover, even if lesbian mothers . . . "other" boy children in the more libidinally neutral sense of perceiving boys' anatomical differentness — where boys' sexual organs are merely different, with no special valences attached to them — it still makes little sense for there to be any "pushing" of sons into oedipal dynamics. Sometimes a penis is just a penis.

You see the kind of multi-layered craziness we're dealing with here? During the course of researching radical feminism, I've gathered dozens of books crammed full of theoretical lunacy like this.

Do I understand "oedipal dynamics" the way a Ph.D. does? Of course not. However, speaking as the father of six children, I don't need any theoretical training to say: *You're crazy!*

You don't have to be able to diagram a sentence to understand plain English, and you don't need to make sense of a phrase like "libidinally tinged oedipal dynamics" to say that "Jill Collins" (a pseudonym for the lesbian who takes showers with the 3-year-old son of her partner) is unlikely to raise a son who is psychologically normal. This doesn't mean "Danny" will grow up to be a serial killer or a transgender porn star, but what is the basic message of lesbian motherhood?

Males are unnecessary and undesirable.

Not for a minute do I doubt that lesbian mothers can raise feminist daughters — lesbian mothers exemplify in their lifestyle what feminism teaches in theory — but it's hard to imagine a boy failing to perceive how his lesbian mother has rejected males, *per se.*

Again, to emphasize, perceiving potential problems is possible even if we stipulate both sides of the basic pro-gay argument about families: Yes, we acknowledge that children of same-sex households can and do live useful and productive lives. Yes, we acknowledge that "normal" families can produce badly broken — indeed, dangerously criminal — offspring. Still, isn't it just common sense to expect that lesbian motherhood would yield non-normal outcomes in terms of the psychological health and sexuality of their children?

Never mind whatever social-science survey data on this topic anyone might cite today. Given the known biases of academia, I am not even slightly surprised by sociologists and psychologists publishing studies that proclaim Everybody's Happy in Gay City.

Let's wait until, say 2063 — when the children born in 2013 are 50 — and compare their life outcomes, particularly in terms of their own marriages and families, before declaring that we know that there are no harms produced by same-sex parenting. (I choose 2013 as the reference point because it was that year, in the *Windsor* decision, that the Supreme Court normalized same-sex marriage.) Even if we don't think that children will be obviously *harmed* by growing up in gay households, however, this doesn't mean that gay parenting is the same as normal parenting. And guess what? The critical praise for Maureen Sullivan's book emphasized this difference:

> "Sullivan makes a compelling argument that lesbian families challenge, at root, the very basis of patriarchal familial norms, and indeed modern notions of biological fixity."
> — Arlene Stein, author of *Sex and Sensibility*

> "Maureen Sullivan's book is a notable document of the quiet social revolution that is producing new forms of the family."
> — R. W. Connell, author of *Gender and Power*

You see that Stein (Professor of Women's and Gender Studies, Rutgers University) and Connell (Professor of Education and Social Work, University of Sydney, Australia) praise this book about lesbian motherhood precisely *because* they view this phenomenon as part of a "social revolution" challenging "patriarchal familial norms."

Just as Joyce Trebilcot was not neutral about lesbianism, neither is Maureen Sullivan's book neutral about lesbian motherhood. Sullivan is as objective about lesbian motherhood as Barack Obama is objective about the Democrat Party. The praise for Sullivan's book reflects the same bias as Trebilcot's ideas about "responsible sexuality" — men *bad*, lesbians *good* – which is to say that its message is the same as feminism in general. Remember that Trebilcot in 1974 argued that "moral concepts," including "notions of justice, equality, and liberty," are more important than "the empirical issue of sex differences . . . in the philosophical discussion of sex roles."

It does not matter, from a feminist perspective, whether men and women are actually different in meaningful ways. For the sake of "moral concepts" — that is to say, intellectual abstractions — *we must pretend that sexual differences don't exist*. However, despite this requisite philosophical commitment to a make-believe game of ignoring real differences between men and women, Trebilcot (and feminists generally) insist that males are distinctly inferior. Males exercise illegitimate power (patriarchy) that is inherently harmful to women. Male power is always selfish and coercive, even where it is not actually violent, so that this harmful patriarchal "control" is used to force or deceive women into heterosexuality. The only possible escape from this male control is for women to become lesbians — preferring female sexual partners as more desirable than male partners, without regard to feminism's philosophical commitment to the belief that there are no *actual* differences between men and women.

If the complex logic of Joyce Trebilcot's feminism makes sense to you, congratulations: You must be a highly distinguished Ph.D.

Or maybe you're just crazy.

CONCLUSION
Fear and Loathing of the Penis

"All women are prisoners and hostages to men's world. Men's world is like a vast prison or concentration camp for women. This isn't a metaphor, it's reality. Each man is a threat. We can't escape men. . . .

"[H]eterosexuality doesn't exist and our 'urges' to bond with [men] emotionally or sexually aren't natural drives but normal PTSD reactions to years of abuse and mind-programming."
— Radical Wind, August 2013

WHEN I THINK BACK ON HOW this project began, I recall the woman whose screed against intercourse (*"PIV is always rape, OK?"*) led me deep into this swamp of radical feminism. It was, however, another rant by that same blogger which made me seriously explore the ideological psychosis of which her rant was a symptom.

"No woman is heterosexual."

That four-word sentence sent me off on an investigation of her sources, especially including Professor Dee Graham, whose 1994 book *Loving to Survive* theorized female heterosexuality as a response to male-inflicted "sexual terror," akin to post-traumatic stress syndrome. Understanding this claim in turn required me to examine the sources cited in Graham's bibliography, including lesbian feminists like Marilyn Frye, Adrienne Rich, Mary Daly, Audre Lorde and Charlotte Bunch. Graham even managed to work in a citation to "Starhawk" (*neé* Miriam Simos), the lesbian feminist who was the founding high priestess of a California-based pagan witchcraft cult known as Reclaiming. From such dubious sources Graham had propounded her theory of sexuality, based in a view of men as violent oppressors and women as victims suffering under tyrannical male supremacy. After several months of further research, I began referring to this feminist worldview as Fear and Loathing of the Penis.

You see this in the counterfactual "rape epidemic" hysteria on college campuses, with activists at Columbia University trying to frighten prospective students — high school kids — with protests about "gender-based violence on campus." Robert Tracinski at the Federalist has examined the possibility that "rape culture" discourse represents "an attempt to create a scapegoat for the emotional dark side of promiscuity."

It is evident that these women's dread and contempt of masculinity arises from specific circumstances. Feminism does not necessarily *cause* women to hate and fear men; feminism is the political *rationalization* of these women's anti-male feelings, permitting them to believe that their own unhappiness is not merely personal. It is the explanatory power of feminist theory that attracts women who do not wish to consider themselves responsible for their misfortunes, disappointments and failures, offering them a convenient scapegoat for their problems: *Patriarchy*.

To give you an idea of what I'm talking about, consider this recent post on Tumblr.com by an Australian woman named Kate:

I think that most of the times I feel afraid of the world, it is because there are men in it.

Men who want to hurt women; men who don't want to hurt women but do not realise that they are doing so anyway; men who don't want to hurt women, but do not care when they do, because whatever they want from the situation is intrinsically more important to them.

Men who you can tell are bad just by looking at them or listening to what they say; men who you instinctively feel could be bad, but you second-guess yourself because you want to believe and trust that they are good; men who you would never guess are bad in any way — whose badness doesn't show for years, and when it does it is near-invisible to anybody else.

Men who make you feel threatened when they don't get their own way; men who lash out and shift the focus when they don't get their own way; men who spin every word when they don't get their own way; men who act like children and make you their mother figure when they don't get their own way; men who control you to get their own way, men who take what they want anyway when they don't get their own way.

Men who do not listen to women's words the same way
they listen to other men's; men who turn you invisible
unless they want to f–k you; men who only want to be your
friend because they want to f–k you; men who call you
'intellectually dishonest' for using emotion and context to
argue a point; men who back you into corners physically,
emotionally, verbally.
Men who call you 'crazy'; 'hormonal'; 'irrational';
'emotional', men who will not allow your anger to be
recognised as a valid emotional response, or your sadness,
your distrust.
Men who make you feel the most loved, safe, and cared for
after they have abused you.
Men who make you question your reality by telling you
with conviction that it is wrong.
Men who take away your sense of independence and self by
controlling your every move, and by telling you a better
way to do every little thing you've taught yourself.
Men who dissolve your self esteem by belittling and
insulting you, and calling you names.
Men who tell you that your reasonable emotional reactions
are abusive, and infringe on their rights to do whatever they
want to do.
Men who do not stop whatever they are doing to you when
you ask.
Men who look you in the eyes and lie to you every day to
protect their double lives.
I am so tired of absorbing all of this.

Who are these men who do these things to Kate? We don't know.

She doesn't name them, but she is apparently surrounded by
them, and we are thus unable to offer any advice or assistance to her.
She is a helpless victim of men — *men! men! men!* — and it would
seem she offers this catalog of masculine "badness" in the
expectation that other women will recognize the pattern. Yet we
might notice how Kate lists men's reactions when they "don't get
their own way," as if she can't see that the entirety of her complaint
involves her own dissatisfaction because she can't get her own way
with them. Men don't behave the way Kate wants them to behave,
men don't say and do things the way Kate wants things to be said
and done, and their failure to live up to her expectations — their

unwillingness to comply with the imperious demands of Queen Kate — is proof that she is a victim of male oppression.

She is inviting us to a pity party where she is the guest of honor. If men reject that invitation, this just proves how bad men are, because they "will not allow your anger to be recognised as a valid emotional response, or your sadness, your distrust."

Why wouldn't male contempt for her be "a valid emotional response"? Men are the way we are in part because we must be that way in order to be recognized as men, as responsible adults. Nobody wants to hear a man complain about his problems. Women can be especially merciless in their contempt for any man who expresses a sense of emotional suffering, and many women are deliberately sadistic toward men. Some women enjoy nothing better than to insult a man and then mock him as a "whiner" if he takes notice of the insult. Women who take pride in their own cruelty toward men are invariably the same women who complain when men fail to treat them with solicitude and kindness. Such women are never able to admit that they are even partially responsible for their inability either to attract good men or to sustain relationships with the men they do attract.

Fear and Loathing of the Penis — a paranoid resentment of men, characterized by irrational suspicion — is the underlying mental condition that feminism turns into a political ideology. What disturbs me, after months of studying this phenomenon, is that this madness is both contagious and incurable. Feminism is a sort of cultural virus that, once it takes hold in a woman's mind, makes it impossible for her to relate to men in a normal manner and, because misery loves company, she feels compelled to share her hateful anti-male attitudes with other women. If left untreated, the effects of this dangerous malady are well known.

> "[Feminism is] a socialist, anti-family political movement that encourages women to leave their husbands, kill their children, practice witchcraft, destroy capitalism and become lesbians."
> – Pat Robertson, 1992

This has become one of the famous statements ever made about feminism, mainly because feminists enjoy quoting it ironically, as if it were self-evidently absurd. Yet what part of it is false? Certainly feminism encourages women to "kill their children" through abortion. The feminist movement is anti-marriage and anti-family, advocating no-fault divorce. Is feminism "socialist," seeking to "destroy capitalism"? Absolutely so – around the world, the feminist movement is associated with left-wing political parties, the Democrats in the United States, Labour in England and Australia, the radical Greens in much of Europe. Modern feminism began with the radical New Left of the 1960s, and the faculties of Women's Studies programs include self-declared socialist feminists like University of Colorado professor Alison Jaggar and University of California-Santa Cruz professor Bettina Aptheker. In fact, Professor Aptheker's biography is nearly a perfect summary of Robertson's quote. She was the daughter of the Communist Party historian Herbert Aptheker. She married a Communist activist named Jack Kurzweil and had two children. They divorced in 1978, and Bettina then moved in with her lesbian lover, Kate Miller, who was also divorced from her husband. Aptheker and Miller raised their three children together and at least one of them, Aptheker's daughter Jenny Kurzweil, grew up to be a lesbian herself.

Feminist women who have divorced their husbands and become lesbians are by no means rare. There are entire books about this phenomenon, including 1995's *From Wedded Wife to Lesbian Life: Stories of Transformation* (edited by Deborah Abbott and Ellen Farmer) and 2010's *Dear John, I Love Jane: Women Write About Leaving Men for Women* (edited by Candace Walsh and Laura Andre). In 2014, Lauren Morelli, a writer for the lesbian-themed TV series *Orange Is the New Black*, made headlines after she divorced her husband and became the lesbian lover of one of the show's stars. The lesbian blog Autostraddle featured an article with the provocative headline "How to Leave Your Husband (Because You're a Lesbian)" written by a woman who divorced the father of her two children after the cable TV show *The L Word* convinced her she was actually a lesbian.

This is by no means a recent phenomenon. In 1980, Australian feminist Denise Thompson described how "countless numbers of lesbians" joined the feminist movement because it offered them "the possibility of a cultural community of women whose primary commitment was to other women rather than to men." Furthermore, Thompson added, the rise of the feminist movement produced a "mass exodus of feminist women from the confining structures of heterosexuality" in such numbers as to raise questions about "the institution of heterosexuality in the consciousness of those feminists who, for whatever reason, chose not to change their sexual orientation." And why shouldn't this have been the expected result?

Women "changed their sexual/social orientation from men to women," Thompson explained, "in response to the feminist political critique of their personal situations of social subordination." If the personal is political (as feminists say) and if women's relationships with men are "confining structures" of "social subordination," why would *any* feminist be heterosexual?

To ask that question, however, suggests the obverse: Why would any heterosexual woman be a feminist? If she genuinely likes men – if she wants to marry a man and a have a family – what could this radical anti-male ideology possibly offer her? It is impossible that any feminist could ever admire, respect or trust any male because, after all, it is men who oppress women, and all men benefit from this oppressive system of patriarchy. In fact, some feminists have argued for the eradication of males. Professor Sally Gearhart wrote in 1982:

> Enslaved by male-identification and years of practice within the system as we all still are to one degree or another, the assumption must be that the present system of monopoly capitalism and patriarchy must be replaced and that non-male-identified women must be the responsible ones. . . .
> At least three further requirements supplement the strategies of environmentalists if we are to create and preserve a less violent world. I) Every culture must begin to affirm a female future. II) Species responsibility must be returned to women in every culture. III) *The proportion of men must be reduced to and maintained at approximately 10% of the human race. . . .*
> To return species responsibility to women means in very practical terms that erotic and reproductive initiative must be restored to women all over the globe. . . . Make the decision entirely that of the woman as to how she will be impregnated and how often, if indeed she chooses to be so at all, and whether by heterosexual intercourse, artificial insemination or a form of ovular merging. Restore to each woman the inalienable right to say what shall become of

any fertilized egg and to control absolutely the number of children she wishes to emerge from her body. . . . Make nonexistent any male's say-so in the process of reproduction. Create and protect alternative structures of economic and psychological support for independent women — women not attached to men — who are child-bearers and child-raisers. . . .

Women will bear the number of children they know can be sustained not just by their own social group but by the wide ecological system. They will not bear the children that some man wants only to perpetuate his name or the family possession of his property; they will not bear the children they presently convince themselves they must have because their only role is obedient wife and mother; women will not have the children men think are necessary to perpetuate the tribe or the religion or the specific culture. Instead they will bear the children that they want, that they can care for, and that they assess are needed by the specific group and the entire species. . . .

In every culture it must be women in charge of the changes: women-identified women, no women who are pawns of men, not women who out of their fear of losing their lives or those of their children, still hold to the securities of that dangerous patriarchal culture, but women utterly free of coercion, free of male influence and committed to the principle that the right of species regulation is their own, and not the prerogative of any man. I suggest that lesbians and other independent women are already moving in this direction. . . .

To secure a world of female values and female freedom we must, I believe, add one more element to the structure of the future: *the ratio of men to women must be radically reduced so that men approximate only ten percent of the total population.* . . .

We now come to a critical point: how is such a reduction in the male population to take place? One option is of course male infanticide. It differs very little from the female infanticide that has apparently been carried out even into the twentieth century by some cultures. Such an alternative

is clearly distasteful and would not constitute creative social change. . . .
[I]f women are given the freedom of their bodies then they may well choose [experimental "ovular merging" technology that produces only female embryos] in great enough numbers to make a significant difference in the sex ratio of women to men. A 75% female to 25% male ratio could be achieved in one generation if one-half of a population reproduced heterosexually and one-half by ovular merging.
Such a prospect is attractive to women who feel that if they bear sons no amount of love and care and nonsexist training will save those sons from a culture where male violence is institutionalized and revered. These are women saying, "No more sons. We will not spend twenty years of our lives raising a potential rapist, a potential batterer, a potential Big Man."

Selective reproductive processes to reduce males to 10 percent of the population? Women who are so hostile to "dangerous patriarchal culture" that they view *their own sons* as potential rapists? What kind of kook would even imagine such things? Professor Gearhart was not an obscure "fringe" figure. She helped establish one of the first Women's Studies programs at San Francisco State University in the 1970s. After her 1979 feminist utopian novel *The Wanderground* (in which a tribe of lesbian separatists have developed the powers of telepathy and telekinesis) was published, Professor Gearheart gave an interview to the lesbian journal *Off Our Backs* in which she praised Wicca, speaking of "women who are doing rituals, who are getting into healing and all that," of "psychic energy" and "healing energy." An online biography notes that Professor Gearhart "was also a leader in the women's spirituality movement." This brings us full circle to the lesbian feminist witchcraft of Starhawk, whose 1979 book *The Spiral Dance* is the most popular book in the history of modern pagan witchcraft.

Starhawk was a follower of Z Budapest (*neé* Zsuzsanna Emese Mokcsay), the founder of what is known as "Dianic Wicca." An immigrant from Hungary, she married and had two sons, but in 1970 joined the feminist movement, divorced her husband and became a lesbian. (Sound familiar?) Moving to Los Angeles, she became a fortune-teller and in 1975, when she was prosecuted under a city ordinance forbidding such activity, she issued a statement declaring her feminist faith:

> I am a witch, worshipping a free goddess who has no traffic
> with men. Diana, the goddess of the wild. The lesbian
> goddess. She who rules over women's mysteries. She who
> is oracular. She who is the soul of nature.
> My coven is the Susan B. Anthony Coven Number One.
> We are a feminist religious group, consciously reclaiming
> the goddess religion for modern wimmin [sic] today.

The publicity resulting from her trial (she was found guilty) helped spread Budapest's "goddess religion," which has become part of a worldwide movement known as "feminist spirituality." Every year, women gather for the International Goddess Festival in a California redwood forest, while in England the Glastonbury Goddess Conference has convened annually for the past 20 years.

This feminist pagan movement founded by the lesbian witch Z Budapest has even begun to influence nominally Christian groups. The ultra-liberal Evangelical Lutheran Church in America (ECLA) has ordained a transgender minister, Rev. Megan Rohrer, who "identifies as butch, dyke, queer, and trans" and in 2014 underwent surgery to have her breasts removed. Before getting her own church, Rohrer was associate pastor at another San Francisco church, Ebenezer Lutheran, known as "Herchurch," an ECLA congregation that promotes goddess worship as "The Divine Feminine," promising to "deconstruct Christianity and other patriarchal religions so that both a new paradigm and worldview may emerge that truly creates an egalitarian, just, society and eco-sensitivies that tend to mending the web of life." At its annual "Faith and Feminism" conference in 2011, this Lutheran church featured meditation led by a self-declared priestess of the Egyptian goddess Isis. In 2013, another ECLA feminist leader, Nadia Bolz-Weber, spoke about her own experiences with Wicca and claimed that the Wiccan goddess is "simply another aspect of the divine."

Women's Studies professors were among those who promoted this modern revival of witchcraft. On Mother's Day 1989, Boston University professor Mary Daly organized a theatrical event she called "The Witches Return" which concluded with the assembled cast on stage chanting, "Power to the witch and to the woman in me!" To understand how witchcraft and feminism intersected, it's helpful to have the testimony of Catherine Telford-Keogh, a young Canadian who in 2013 received a master's degree in Women, Gender and Sexuality Studies from Yale University. In a 2010 essay entitled "Queering Feminist Witchcraft," Telford-Keogh says she felt that the Christian church in which she was raised "did not speak to my experiences as a woman questioning her identity and sexuality":

> What first interested me in Witchcraft was this challenging of the patriarchal heterosexual construction of what it means to be a woman. ... I enrolled in a class at [the University of Waterloo, Ontario] entitled "Women and the Great Religions" and became acquainted with Goddess Centered Feminist Witchcraft. I found this tradition fascinating as it addressed and centrally focused on the rejection of patriarchal constructions of womanhood. Goddess Centered Feminist Witchcraft emerged as part of the Feminist Spirituality Movement in the 1970s, during the second wave feminist movement. ... Goddess Centered Feminist Witchcraft constructs the divine as female identified, drawing on elements of goddess worship across cultures and religious traditions and places women's experiences, such as menstruation and childbirth, at the center of spiritual practice. ... It also affirms that goddess-worshipping cultures existed at the advent of civilization and were eventually overtaken by the global shift toward patriarchy revealing the naturalness of patriarchy as a falsity.

Alas, it appears that Telford-Keogh has been misled. The belief in a prehistoric matriarchal past, promoted by devotees of Wicca, has been discredited by anthropologists, archaeologists and historians. Like so much else crucial to the feminist worldview, claims about ancient women-dominated cultures had no firm basis in factual evidence. Wishful thinking and careless interpretation of a few pieces of Neolithic art gave rise to this myth of ancient matriarchies. British historian Ronald Hutton has described the claims made by Jaquetta Hawkes, who promoted the "Great Goddess" mythology in the 1940s and 1950s:

> New Stone Agers were woman-centered, peaceful, creative, and living in harmony with Nature, worshipped as a single goddess. This happy religion had united the whole of

114

Europe from one end of the continent to the other until
destroyed by patriarchal invaders worshipping sky gods.

Attributing such wondrous qualities to people of the Neolithic past was, of course, a means of criticizing the modern world. False nostalgia for an imaginary non-existent matriarchal past is no more helpful than dreams of a utopian feminist future where, as Professor Gearhart imagined, lesbians would be endowed with magical powers of telekinesis and telepathy. As pleasant as these dreams may be to those who dream them, they are likely to produce nightmares if we attempt to implement them here in the real world. And this is the great danger, because feminists refuse to recognize that their theories of an androgynous regime of "sexual equality" where normal gender roles have been abolished are incompatible with the reality of human nature.

It is a foolish mistake to quote Pat Robertson's 1992 description of feminism as a joke. As we have seen, every single word of it is true, including the crazy-sounding part about feminism encouraging women to "practice witchcraft ... and become lesbians." Of course, most feminists are neither witches nor lesbians – not yet, anyway. If we look back over recent decades, however, we cannot underestimate how much further damage feminists might inflict in their effort to destroy our civilization in the name of "equality."

Human nature cannot be eradicated by ideology. Yet feminists have obtained immense political power and cultural influence, and the ways in which they use that power and influence to change laws, policies, customs and beliefs will have an impact on the lives of millions of ordinary people who have not asked for their opinions, people who have no idea what plans these radicals have for them and their children.

Feminists have very *interesting* plans for your children. In February 2015, Barnard College's Center for Research on Women announced an "Action on Education" conference that featured a panel:

Dreams of Feminist Education
Tadashi Dozono, Ileana Jiménez, Cheyenne Tobias
Two teachers of color, both feminist and queer, will share
their dreams for feminist education in schools. Moving
from theory to action, Ileana and Tadashi work alongside
their students using various feminisms such as women of

color feminism, global feminism, trans-feminism and queer theory. Their pedagogical practices incorporate restorative and social justice, inspiring innovative curricula that are intersectional and interdisciplinary. In collaboration with Cheyenne Tobias, feminist artist and Ileana's former student, Tadashi and Ileana will bring us on a visual journey through two different school contexts via the successes they've had and the challenges they face in bringing a feminist vision to their respective classrooms. Calling us to action through their own personal storytelling, Ileana and Tadashi will urge us to consider the role of feminism in schools and the role that schools play in feminism.

What kind of lessons do these self-described queer feminists want to teach your children? Would it be paranoid to suspect that these lessons might involve destroying capitalism and practicing witchcraft? If radical theories are embraced and promoted at elite institutions like Barnard College (where tuition for the 2014-2015 school year was $46,040), shouldn't we expect that there will be an intellectual trickle-down effect, so that these feminist ideas about "social justice" are diffused into the K-12 curriculum? If parents do not "share their dreams for feminist education in schools," what can be done to prevent these queer feminists from teaching their "inspiring innovative curricula" to future generations?

The question of what can be done to stop this feminist agenda is one that is not easily answered, except to say what I have already said: *All that is necessary to defeat feminism is to tell the truth about feminism.*

We should never underestimate the common sense of the American people. If the good and decent citizens of our country learn the truth about feminism, we need not doubt they will oppose it. Unfortunately, feminists are determined to conceal the truth, to continue hiding behind glittering generalities – vague slogans about "equality" and "progress" – using accusations of "misogyny" and "bigotry" to silence those opponents who dare to tell the truth. Many people are confused by these deceptions, and don't want to believe that their children are targets of indoctrination.

"In the hands of a skillful indoctrinator, the average student not only thinks what the indoctrinator wants him to think . . . but is altogether positive that he has arrived at his position by independent intellectual exertion. This man is outraged by the suggestion that he is the flesh-and-blood tribute to the success of his indoctrinators."

– William F. Buckley Jr., *Up From Liberalism* (1959)

Our ability to resist this kind of indoctrination – to be able to see through the efforts of those who want to tell us what to think – requires us to adopt a profound skepticism toward the intellectual elite who promote ideas that contradict our own experiences, our own knowledge, our own common sense. We can see the effects of feminist teaching – deranged women ranting on the Internet about being "prisoners and hostages" in "a vast prison or concentration camp," viewing every man as a "threat" to their survival. We may sympathize with such women, whose minds have been shattered by their unfortunate experiences, but we understand that feminism cannot solve their problems. Yet the philosophy of feminism provides a convenient rationalization of women's unhappiness by attributing all their problems to "patriarchy" and "misogyny," and it is easier for many women to accept that ready-made explanation than to view their problems in terms of individual responsibility. Seldom do these unhappy feminists pause to wonder whether the problems they experience are, in fact, products of feminism's "success." People who attempt to live their lives in accordance with the abstract theories of intellectuals are often surprised to learn the lessons that Rudyard Kipling ascribed to "The Gods of the Copybook Headings":

When the Cambrian measures were forming,
They promised perpetual peace.
They swore, if we gave them our weapons, that the wars of the tribes would cease.
But when we disarmed
They sold us and delivered us bound to our foe,
And the Gods of the Copybook Headings said:
"Stick to the Devil you know."

On the first Feminian Sandstones we were promised the
Fuller Life
(Which started by loving our neighbour and ended by
loving his wife)
Till our women had no more children and the men lost
reason and faith,
And the Gods of the Copybook Headings said:
"The Wages of Sin is Death."

Ancient wisdom endures because human nature is a permanent fact
of life. We cannot reinvent ourselves and reorganize the world to fit
the dreams and schemes of radical intellectuals. There is more truth
to be learned from the Proverbs of Solomon and the Psalms of David
than we could ever possibly learn from the intellectuals who gather
at elite colleges to "share their dreams for feminist education." Yet
all of the resources and prestige of academia are on one side of this
struggle for the future, and those of us who are on the other side
know that our opposition will earn us only the hatred and contempt
of those who earn their living by promoting the elite worldview. We
must therefore begin with a determination to tell the truth despite
every effort to intimidate us into silence, remembering God's
commandment to the ancient Israelites:

"See, I have set before thee this day life and good,
and death and evil . . . I call heaven and earth to
record this day against you, that I have set before
you life and death, blessing and cursing: therefore
choose life, that both thou and thy seed may live . .
."
– Deuteronomy 30:15-19 (KJV)

We must choose life and, having made our choice, we must pray for
divine protection in our struggle again the forces of Death and Evil.
You may not believe in witchcraft, but the witches do. And when
feminists gather in their covens, you can be sure they are not praying
to the God of Life and Good.

Made in the USA
Lexington, KY
01 March 2015